Exploring Humor in Child Welfare Casework

Exploring Humor in Child Welfare Casework

Laugh to Get through It or Cry Forever

Lisa N. Landram and Christian A. Vaccaro

LEXINGTON BOOKS
Lanham • Boulder • New York • London

Published by Lexington Books
An imprint of The Rowman & Littlefield Publishing Group, Inc.
4501 Forbes Boulevard, Suite 200, Lanham, Maryland 20706
www.rowman.com

86-90 Paul Street, London EC2A 4NE

British Library Cataloguing in Publication Information Available

Library of Congress Cataloging-in-Publication Data

Names: Landram, Lisa N., author. | Vaccaro, Christian, author. Title: Exploring humor in
child welfare casework : laugh to get through it   or cry forever / Lisa N. Landram and
Christian A. Vaccaro. Description: Lanham : Lexington Books, [2024] | Includes biblio-
graphical   references and index. | Summary: "This book explores how gallows humor
is used among child welfare caseworkers and what the use of humor, and   gallows
humor, reveals about how employees experience stress and manage   their emotions"--
Provided by publisher. Identifiers: LCCN 2024007736 | ISBN 9781666904369 (cloth) |
ISBN   9781666904376 (ebook) Subjects: LCSH: Child welfare workers--Psychology.
| Child welfare   workers--Job stress | Secondary traumatic stress. | Black   humor-
-Psychological aspects. | Job stress. Classification: LCC HV713 .L36 2024 | DDC 362.7-
-dc23/eng/20240313 LC record available at https://lccn.loc.gov/2024007736

Dedication

This book is dedicated to all the social workers and frontline responders who spend their careers serving others. It is with much gratitude that we dedicate this book to each of you for your selfless and supportive ways. Your hard work and dedication to others does not go unnoticed. As each of you manage your emotions related to your career, we hope that you find comfort through connections with social workers in this book, as well as an understanding of how you are coping with stress and managing emotions.

This book is also dedicated to the numerous administrators in organizations that employ social workers and frontline responders. Without your leadership, programs to aid the community would not be possible. We are optimistic that this book can help you evaluate your organization and your employees to ensure a thriving agency and well cared for staff. We are thankful for you and the organizations you lead.

It is our hope that this book provides knowledge, assistance, policy implementation, and comfort for social workers, frontline responders, and organizations that employ them. May this book also lift your spirits through many giggles and chuckles as you relate to the predicaments that social workers find themselves in. Embrace your sense of humor with joy and an understanding for how to use it wisely and ethically. Happy reading.

Contents

Chapter 1

Stuck in a Police Car

It is like any other day, as a child welfare caseworker, you are sitting at your desk minding your own business, trying to get caught up on the endless mounds of paperwork. Every time your boss walks by, you try to slouch down in your chair and hide, thinking maybe they will not see me. Maybe, they will give the next case to someone else. Surely my boss knows how backed up I am on paperwork and will not give me another case. However, your disappearing act does not work and here comes your supervisor walking your way. Before your mind can wander too much longer your supervisor is in front of you explaining your next assignment. Your mind races thinking about what information is on that sheet of paper, known as the "referral."

Phoebe, an intake child welfare caseworker for nine years and treatment caseworker for one year, recalls a specific case that took her from the comforts of her office chair. Here it was, another new referral being delivered her way. At first, she may have thought to herself that this was like so many of the other referrals she has experienced; that it probably contains misinformation, and the investigation would be a waste of her time. For many child welfare caseworkers, the information from referrals is incorrect, often containing wrong names and addresses. For some social workers, the embarrassment of showing up to a home and asking for wrong names leads to feelings of self-consciousness and concerns of looking unprofessional to the public. Incorrect information on a referral can turn a one-hour job into an all-day affair, as you search for the missing information or the correct home to investigate. An investigation often takes caseworkers down dirty, remote, dead-end roads in the middle of what seems to be nowhere. These trips can be a little harrowing as the roads often evoke the same feelings and imagery as they do when they appear in the common "jump scare" horror movie you have watched. Let's say by some chance the referral contains correct information and you do arrive at the right location with the right names. Often, the caseworker is thrust into family or neighbor feuds whereby the reported allegations are tied into messy disputes where neighbors or ex-partners are accused

1

of using reports to the child welfare system as a form of punishment. Or, as in some referrals, the information is correct, and the allegations are proven to be factual. "Oh, please don't let it be the truth," you might say to yourself as the facts of abuse start to become clearer. But if it is, maybe you will find comfort with the idea that this investigation will lead to the end of unjust behavior to a child, and you get to play a role in saving at least one person. That's a story you can get behind, one where you are a hero saving one life at a time. But even this is slowly met with the sobering fact that you still have paperwork at the office and this case will be added to the pile for a while. It is like you have been slapped in the face with the realization the more time you spend in the field, the more difficult bureaucratic work you will have. Moreover, you are a human being who is experiencing a range of emotions—many of which are negative—this whole time. So, what are you to do with all those pesky emotions that seem to get in the way?

Caseworkers can experience a variety of negative emotions related to what they witness. However, fear plagues your mind. Fear for your own safety. Fear of the danger the child could be in. Fear of what you will personally be exposed to. You start to prepare yourself for the worst. Do you have the right shoes on if you need to run? Will angry parents scream at you and try to fight you? How will you maintain a neutral and calm environment no matter what dilemma you face? If you are not fearful, will you be overwhelmed with sadness? If you are, how do you hold back the tears and remain professional? And if you do manage to suppress your feelings until later, will you be depressed for days at home? Will those close to you ask you again, what is wrong with you? Feeling hopeless by the awareness that even if you did want to talk about it with family and friends, you could not tell them due to confidentiality. Which could cause you to break down or isolate yourself from others all together. Will anyone ever understand you anyway? How do you deal with all of this? What other emotions may you experience? Will you be angry at the parents for the harm they are causing the child? If you are, how do you look past that and help the family? The *what ifs* and unknowns can be stressful and cause a variety of emotions, even before your work with the family ever begins. Not to mention your personal life. Oh yeah, what about those responsibilities? You must pick your child up from daycare by 5:00 pm. Or you have a dinner date. Or you just want to eat at a normal scheduled time, as your stomach so kindly reminds you with a grumble. Will you be late again? Will the daycare charge you again for being late? Should you call someone else to get your child? Should you cancel your date? You search your car for any sort of food that can tie you over until you can get home. Then guilt sits in, and you start to assess your own shortcomings and abilities as a parent, friend, lover, or overall human being. None the less, you find yourself driving to the home to investigate the referral. You are only borrowing trouble, as so many wise ones have said to you. After all, you signed up for this job, didn't you?

So back to Phoebe. Like many child welfare workers, she set out to investigate the new referral. For this case, she was accompanied by another child welfare worker named Dani, which is not always common due to low staffing. She searched for the location not knowing what the area would look like. Her thoughts and emotions start racing. Will she have to drive down a dirt road in the middle of nowhere? Will her car even make it? Or will it be in the city, and she will not be able to find any nearby parking? Does she need to try to park her car in a way she can make a quick getaway if she encounters danger? Will the weather impact her endeavor? Who knows? For now, she just needs to concentrate on finding the place. Having another caseworker along with her helped her clear some of her intrusive thoughts and feelings.

Phoebe and Dani arrived at the referral address, which was a mobile home in a rural part of the county. As they stepped out of her car and into the unknown, Phoebe assessed the surroundings, checking for signs to ensure her own safety as well as making observations for her investigation. She then started to walk her way to the front door with her coworker. She does not know what she will find behind the door. This part of the job always reminds her of the guessing part of the game show "Let's Make a Deal." However, unlike the show, Phoebe doesn't get a choice of what door to look behind or what the surprise will be. She knocks and finds when the door opens that the entire family is home, the birth mother, birth father, and the teenage girl for which the referral was made.

As the investigation proceeds, she and her partner confirm several concerns for the adolescent's welfare. While investigating the concerns in the referral, Phoebe and Dani find themselves in a nasty dilemma that is common in Children and Youth Services, CYS, casework. They must keep from gagging on an intense putrid smell which permeates the entire trailer and will cling to their clothing and hair once they leave. Encountering this smell is a semi-regular occurrence that new social workers must adjust quickly to once in the field. Some social workers refer to it simply as the "client smell," even though using this terminology with outsiders is nearly universally frowned upon as unethical. Experiencing the smell is so common that social workers view it as part of their shared experience. The smell is hard to describe but often comes from a varied combination of sources including cigarette and drug residues, soiled rugs and furniture, molds and mildew, feces and urine, body odors, and spoiled food. Caseworkers typically refrain from acknowledging the smell while at the referral site, recognizing that it accompanies the multifaceted conditions of poverty that are beyond the control of the client. For instance, the family did not have any running water, heat, or electricity in the trailer. Some caseworkers prefer the burning watery eyes from menthol and camphor from putting Vicks under their nose. This tactic helps to mask the offending smells, attenuate disgusted facial expressions, present them as neutral, and remain professional.

Along with keeping expressions of disgust from the smell to themselves on the job, caseworkers certainly don't mention their regular experience of it to those outside of the field. There is a stigma from it. A fear of others' perceptions of them. As if a job that involves regularly encountering this smell might lead to their diminishment as professionals.

Along with the smell comes other concerns of disease and parasites that caseworkers also try to quietly address without causing offense. For instance, some caseworkers coat their hair with hairspray in an effort to protect against acquiring lice. To avoid bringing home roaches or other pests, caseworkers avoid putting their bags or anything else down on the ground. Or you simply do not carry your purse into the home. Regardless of how a caseworker decides to address the physical experience they have from the smell or the other conditions of the home, they must mask their own perceptions and physical experiences during their investigation.

There Phoebe and Dani were at the referral home, as prepared as caseworkers can be for this type of situation. During their interview, Phoebe and her coworker learned that the birth father had a shed in the back of the home that he primarily used to cook methamphetamines. Methamphetamine is an amphetamine-type stimulant whose use has grown epidemic across the United States and many other parts of the world (Maxwell, 2005). It is commonly referred to as meth or crystal. Making meth consists of combing and heating chemical compounds that produce hazardous byproducts and create safety concerns. It is common that the physical health of others is impacted by the process of cooking meth. Therefore, a caseworker would have concerns for the well-being of a child beyond the parents' use of this drug and extending to their proximity of its production is exposing them to physical and environmental harm. Even beyond this, a caseworker would be considered in danger by just being around the production of meth during the investigation. You can imagine that Phoebe's thoughts about her own safety and exposure would be at the forefront of her mind. Am I safe? Do I need to tell my supervisor and make a doctor's visit because of the exposure? Is this referral putting my family at risk? However, for the time being, you realize that right now you cannot think about yourself. You need to ensure this child is safe, and then, only then can you start to go down the rabbit hole of your own demise.

While the caseworkers were in the home, their investigation uncovered the fact that the child's parents were providing her with drugs and alcohol. They also noted that the parents would involve the child in their own use by having her "hold a meth pipe for her mom" so the birth mother could smoke meth.

When the caseworker team found drug paraphernalia in the teen's room, the family turned on them. They began accusing Phoebe and Dani of planting it. Imagine. As if the investigation of drug manufacturing at the home and use involving the teen were not stressful enough issues to address, now the caseworkers had to deal with an increasingly angry family that was attacking their professional character. Yet, caseworkers are expected to remain professional with their clients even under this type of pressure. Remember that Phoebe and Dani are also human, so remaining calm is no small task when feeling frustrated and annoyed at being attacked. Despite the hostility from the family, they persisted with the investigative tasks on the referral.

In the investigation, the caseworkers noted that the birth mother was severely handicapped and had no way to care for herself. They first found her emaciated and lying on a couch with a sheet covering her entire body. She wasn't moving and initially she didn't even appear to be breathing. You can only imagine Phoebe's and Dani's thoughts in overdrive. Was mother dead? Several emotions coursed through Phoebe's body—shock, fear, and horror. This tension was broken by relief when Phoebe saw the sheet move and understood that she had not just discovered a corpse, but a person in a methamphetamine-induced stupor. Ultimately, Phoebe called an ambulance to the home to get the woman medical help because she was not too far away from dying from malnourishment and exposure.

There were also concerns noted in the referral that the teen has been truant from school. If Phoebe and Dani did not address that issue school administrators might lodge a status offense court complaint. In Phoebe's mind, this was not a big issue compared to the other issues but not addressing it would add fuel to the common opinion that child welfare workers could not fix issues. When Phoebe interviewed her, the teen could not discern a clear reason as to why she had missed so much school. Yet, as a seasoned caseworker could only presume it has something to do with the drug usage in the home and this underlying issue was more concerning at the time. In fact, Phoebe and Dani concluded that there were compounding issues all occurring at once with the case, that likely needed to be addressed at the same time. Phoebe explained that the first meeting of the investigation was a long day for her and her coworker. As a result, they ended up outside of the trailer for the next six hours sorting everything out with other responders.

The referral led to the police and the EMS being called to the scene, and this meant additional time and effort for Phoebe and Dani to direct the referral specifics. The winter weather was so frigid it made for an almost unbearably slow passage of time. But the child welfare caseworkers were required to wait on the scene for the situation to be resolved. The police showed kindness to Phoebe and Dani by offering them a seat in the back of the cruiser to warm up. So, there it was, Phoebe and Dani found themselves waiting and thinking about how this was the last place they thought they would end up today.

After warming up, they knew it was time to get back on the scene and finish addressing the concerns in the referral they had for the family. They went to lift the handle of the door to get out of the police car only to realize the door was locked. As if they needed another issue to deal with today. Phoebe recounted that Dani and she were trying to not "cry" or "flip out" about being locked in the car, and at this near breaking point is when the joking and laughing started. Phoebe and Dani first started to giggle and then hysterically laughed until tears poured down their faces. Laughter was their way of relieving all the stress that was unfolding that day. As they laughed, they felt such a release of the negative emotions that built up over such a dreadful and tragic situation. Phoebe recalled that during the investigation she experienced "a lot of emotions" and she felt "really bad" about the whole situation and its complexities. But somehow, the humor in it all made for a needed temporary relief. Her and Dani turned from joking about being locked in the police cruiser to the family's accusation of them of planting drugs in their home. They mimicked the absurdity of the accusation, "I carry meth around on me all the time to plant [on clients]." They laughed at the fact that being put in the back of a police car was a nice setting after everything else they were exposed to in the investigation. They chose to laugh about it, what else could they do when faced with this new predicament they were in? Humor allowed them to brush off their feelings and provided space for them to brainstorm on how to deal with their new situation and move forward so they can ensure that the teen in the referral was safe. All while tamping down their negative feelings about being cold, dealing with the wicked problems of poverty, being accused of planting drugs, and getting stuck in the back of a police car. Spoiler alert, they did get out.

Phoebe and Dani are not unique, as we have learned for most caseworkers the use of humor to self-regulate emotions when placed in difficult situations and interacting with troublesome people ends up being a common and essential tool to perform their job effectively. Child welfare caseworkers regularly interact with clients in the community that have behavioral and emotional troubles and are put into odd and difficult situations and contexts as well. These types of conditions create a variety of dilemmas, stressors, and emotions for caseworkers in which they utilize—for better or worse—humor to address.

The Office of Children, Youth and Families

The Office of Children, Youth and Families is the first federal agency within the U.S. Government—and in fact, the world—to focus exclusively on improving the lives of children and families" (Children's Bureau: An Office of the Administration for Children & Families, 2019, p. 1). The Office of Children, Youth and Families is institutionally located within the broader system of child welfare. "The child welfare system is a group of services designed to promote the well-being of children by ensuring safety, achieving permanency, and strengthening families to care for their children successfully" (Child Welfare Information Gateway, 2013, p. 1). This system is composed of a variety of organizations and people that seek to assist families and ensure the protection of children. Each U.S. state government has its own configuration of organizations that are primarily responsible for the welfare of children (Child Welfare Information Gateway, 2013). Additionally, each U.S. County has its own unique variation of Child Welfare System organizations. Some organizations are named after the county they reside in, followed by the title Office of Children, Youth and Families or Children and Youth Services. These local organizations receive federal direction from the Office of Children, Youth and Families, which is responsible for executing the federal child and family legislation laws (Child Welfare Information Gateway, 2013). "The Office of Children, Youth and Families" is situated under the "Administration on Children, Youth and Families, Administration for Children and Families," and the "U.S. Department of Health and Human Services" (Child Welfare Information Gateway, 2013, p. 2).

Within each county, the Office of Children, Youth and Families is the unit that receives referrals for allegations of possible abuse and then investigates the referral for alleged child abuse and neglect. After a referral of allegations is accepted for investigation and assessed, then corrective and support services may be provided to assist the family. In some cases, Office of Children, Youth and Families employees are required to work with other organizations to assist the family (Child Welfare Information Gateway, 2019). If it is deemed through the agency and the court system that the child(ren), being helped, are still not safe in their home, then arrangements are made for the child(ren) to live with a kinship parent(s) or foster parent(s). During the child(ren)'s placement, the parents or guardians work to meet goals set for reunification. If reunification is not met, then the Office of Children, Youth and Families will arrange for the child(ren) to have permanency in another setting. Figure 1 provides an overview of the referral process within the Office of Children, Youth and Families.

Office of Children, Youth and Families organizational structure consists of a line-level of intake caseworkers and treatment caseworkers. Above them are managerial supervisors and administrative staff employed at each agency. There are also typically auxiliary employees that include lawyers, paralegals, clerical workers, and fiscal workers. Many agencies include specialized line-level workers such as those that focus on foster care placements or independent living.

Our focus for this book is on the line-level intake department and treatment department child welfare caseworkers. Intake caseworkers are the first to respond to allegations of abuse. Just like in the story of Phoebe and Dani, they assess the allegations in referrals, then if the family needs more therapeutic services the case becomes active with a treatment caseworker. After the investigation is completed, treatment caseworkers assist the family in meeting goals—including those for reunification. Some agencies refer to the departments by different names, such as assessment (intake) and ongoing (treatment). In our book, we refer to the two departments with two separate types of caseworkers as intake and treatment. Some agencies (typically smaller in size) have general caseworkers that do the intake investigation and then provide treatment services to the client. As a routine part of employment, all caseworkers are exposed to contexts and situations like Phoebe and Dani, which cause stress and negative emotion. Our research finds that in most cases we encountered, line-level intake and treatment child welfare caseworkers utilize humor as a response.

DR. LANDRAM'S BACKGROUND

In qualitative research, it is not as easy for the researcher to remain an aloof observer since it requires close interactions with participants. Therefore, researchers need to recognize their role and be cognizant of what the participant is saying (Smith, 1990, 2007). Researchers should be aware of how their own experiences inform the way they interpret information (Creswell, 2009) and should be honest in their reporting it so that others can take their research findings together with their positionality.

In this line, it is important to note that, the first author (Dr. Landram) has been employed both as an intake child protective caseworker and an intake supervisor. She has also worked for a provider of the Office of Children, Youth and Families, facilitating adoptions. Dr. Landram has her own experiences with managing negative emotions and stress by using humor throughout her employment with the Office of Children, Youth and Families. When Dr. Landram was an intake caseworker and supervisor, she often observed caseworkers make meaning of their emotions and stress and attempt to manage their emotions and stressors through humor. One responsibility as supervisor was to read all the reports that the caseworkers would generate. By simply reading about the abuses uncovered from the referrals, Dr. Landram could see the various challenges faced by her caseworkers on the frontline. Reports commonly included harrowing details of children's experiences of

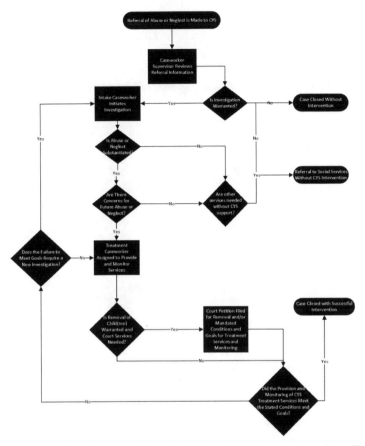

Figure 1.1. The referral process within the Office of Children, Youth and Families.

abuse and horrendous accounts of the guardian's emotions and behaviors. In her time as a supervisor, she became increasingly concerned about the well-being of caseworkers and began to see how these experiences were connected to patterns of caseworkers deflecting emotions. For example, they would argue with each other, drink alcohol in their free time, regularly cry in the office, and even avoid doing employee tasks.

Some caseworkers—even ones with high capability—would regularly quit their positions due to the pressures of stress and emotions. Of course, there are always multiple reasons given for resignation, but in most emotional burnout was a common underlying factor. Many staff would transfer to other line-level departments or try alternative shifts in hopes of finding relief, only to report the same persistent stressors and negative emotions in their new role or shift. When capable staff would burn out and leave, this increased the burden on the child protective caseworkers that remained.

Dr. Landram started to notice a few common coping methods among the caseworkers that were able to continue working without burning out. A group of long-term employees were a part of a beer club that spent the weekends together trading beer and sharing stories. Other resilient caseworkers developed relationships at work with others where they could be trusted to debrief stressful cases. Dr. Landram found that both used forms of humor and in particular "dark" gallows humor to expose a funny side to the horrific situations that they experienced.

Dr. Landram began to make connections with what was going on in the office to the ways she used humor in her childhood to cope with difficulties and to manage her emotions when situations were beyond her control. She also remembers how she used humor as a tool for recognition as a teenager. She realized how much she enjoyed laughing and joking as a form of simple entertainment, as well. She thought about how many times she used humor as an adult to bond with others, bring joy to conversations and to cope with stress and manage emotions.

She found that office coworkers were doing this for the same purposes except under the context that they were dealing with traumatic situations. This was a way for coworkers to connect and feel at ease about their situation. For better and worse, humor was a tool used to attempt to lighten the heaviness of the horrific situations that all employees were dealing with.

Dr. Landram found herself trying to make sense of the environment and how factors connected to each other. This was like no other environment she had been exposed to before and employees were acting in ways she had never seen individuals act before. One area that particularly stood out to her was the appeal of gallows humor in talking about tragic and disturbing situations as a relieving, cathartic, and exhilarating "pressure release valve."

THE PROBLEM

Office of Children, Youth and Families employees regularly experience intense negative emotions and stressors related to their employment. Child welfare employees have persistent exposure to stressful situations, which can lead to emotional exhaustion (Johnco, Salloum, Olson & Edwards, 2014). This is evident in the high staff turnover rates among caseworkers (Salloum, Kondrat, Johnco & Olson, 2015), low salaries (Salloum et al., 2015), high caseloads, (Stalker, Mandell, Frensch, Harvey & Wright, 2007), job-related task stressors and a stressful working environment (Anderson, 2000). Furthermore, employees struggle to keep apprised of and trained according to the continuous changes in child welfare laws and organizational policies.

As such employees are under the added pressure of ensuring that they are following the rules, which creates an ongoing learning curve.

The nature of work puts child welfare employees at risk for their own safety, which is a persistent concern among caseworkers (Stalker et al., 2007). Child protective workers are at an increased risk of violence from the clients they serve compared to other human service workers (Shin, 2011). Employees also struggle with structural constraints in job roles and have difficulty managing stress, which leads to additional conflict. Caseworkers often have conflict over the management of cases due to their assigned tasks as an intake or treatment caseworker. For instance, intake employees confront clients with allegations of abuse, while treatment employees attempt to assist families to alleviate concerns. All these experiences and factors contribute to stress and impact employee emotions. Employees are also addressing situations and dilemmas that can produce several emotions.

During employment, Office of Children, Youth and Families employees are exposed to a high degree of situations around neglect and physical and sexual abuse of children that cue intense emotional responses in both the caseworker and referred family (Anderson, 2000). Since caseworkers and supervisors solve family problems and address allegations within referrals, families and guardians of children can become frustrated with the allegations against them, which makes work difficult for employees. Similarly, employees can be emotionally shocked by the situations and details of abuse that they encounter and become emotionally exhausted from these interactions, which can impact their work (Taris & Schreurs, 2009). Child protective investigators experience anger, depression, uneasiness, guilt, loneliness, helplessness, and disappointment in their work (Howell, 2008). As a result, employees manage their own emotions and feelings while they assist families, and depending on how they do this, the quality of services to the families potentially suffers (Heverling, 2011).

To manage these emotions, employees utilize negative and positive coping mechanisms in combination to address stress and emotions related to work duties (Farester, 2016; Heverling, 2011). For example, an employee may choose to spend one-fourth of their time drinking alcohol heavily (a negative coping strategy), while also choosing to spend three-fourths of their time venting with other employees (a positive coping strategy) and as a form of social connection. Heverling's (2011) research reveals that some child welfare workers utilize negative coping mechanisms, which can include a change in eating patterns and/or drinking alcohol and smoking. These behaviors harm personal relationships and can influence employee burnout (Heverling, 2011). However, some child welfare employees use positive coping mechanisms such as physical activity, maintaining a sense of humor, venting, communicating, and the utilization of relaxation techniques (Heverling, 2011).

These coping mechanisms help Office of Children, Youth and Families employees address experiences they have with stress and emotions related to their employment, that directly impacts their employee outcomes and the organization's mission. Stress has effects on Office of Children, Youth and Families employees individually, as a group and on the environment and culture they are working in. Conrad and Kellar-Guenther's (2006) research suggest that child welfare employees need social support and need to process traumatic events that occur daily to become successful at managing their stress and emotions associated with their employment. Therefore, organizational leaders need to understand how employees experience stress and emotions in the workplace. One unique way they can examine this is to look at the types of humor used among employees. Humor can be used for coping (Johnson, 2007) because it's a means for "constantly changing cognitive and behavioral efforts to manage specific external and/or internal demands that are appraised as taxing or exceeding the person's resources" (Lazarus & Folkman, 1984, as cited in Folkman, Lazarus, Dunkel-Schetter, DeLongis & Gruen, 1986, p. 993).

The study of humor can point to sources of stress and how employees manage stress and intrusive emotion. Humor also provides a mechanism for social support (Turcotte, 2017) as groups attempt to manage emotions after traumatic events. Humor is also a source of social control (Obrdlik, 1942). Therefore, the study of humor in employee groups can uncover how emotions and stress are managed. Taken together, the study of humor in an organization can reveal overall weaknesses and strengths in an organization and provide insight to leaders for changes needed in their agency. Furthermore, humor is an organizational tool that may be harnessed by leaders as a resource to help employees manage stressors and emotions and reduce compassion fatigue, secondary trauma, and burnout. To summarize, a better understanding of humor and gallows humor is needed to help employees individually, as a group, and to assist the organization in meeting its mission.

CONTRIBUTIONS TO RESEARCH

This study contributes to social sciences research in several ways. First by extending knowledge on theories of humor, stress, and the sociology of emotions. This research also contributes to the development of research on gallows humor where a paucity of research currently exists. It also provides a study of child welfare employees that utilize humor, while assessing job roles through the lens of humor theory, gallows humor, stress theory and the sociology of emotions. Here, past research mostly focused on humor and stress, but there are also some studies on humor and the sociology of emotions. This research can aid in that area and provides data that can help better understand how all three theories connect to one another. This includes incorporating concepts from the stress process model and job strain. This can help to better understand the use of humor within the Office of Children, Youth and Families and how it may connect to stress. Craun and Bourke's (2014, 2015) research assesses the association of different types of humor and stress and notes some associations. Vivona (2014) assesses humor in the workplace of law enforcement employees and noted that humor reduces stress and addresses emotional burdens. These studies mention that emotions can be stressful; however, there is little mention of the core concepts of the sociology of emotions. Thus, this is an area of research that can be developed more and can further the knowledge of stress, humor, emotion management and labor.

Emotion Management and Employee Roles

Emotion management is an interactive process where individuals do "work" to bring emotions in line with the contexts they are in (Hochschild, 1979). It is an interactive process that attempts to change the degree or kind of emotions or feelings one experiences (Hochschild, 2003). Generating humor, which involves a group dynamic to make something comic or amusing, can be used as a form of emotion management. Emotional labor is the process of emotion management as an aspect of their work, which is required by Office of Children, Youth and Families caseworkers. Our research assists in understanding humor impacts on employee stress, client interactions, and job performance in two caseworker roles (intake caseworker and treatment caseworker).

Our study is modeled after Hochschild's (2003) landmark book, *The Managed Heart,* which examines emotional labor among bill collectors and flight attendants. Although both engage in emotional labor and utilize the similar processes to regulate them against emotional rules, the flight attendants' emotional labor had the effect of enhancing the status of their customers while the emotional labor of bill collectors has the effect of diminishing the status of their payees. Hochschild (2003) showed how this difference was due to their employee role.

Even though the Office of Children, Youth and Families have the same mission and expectations for their employees, each job-related task and department have different employee roles and experiences that translate to different relationships with their clients and therefore different emotional labor. For instance, intake caseworkers investigate referrals and determine abuse and treatment caseworkers providing therapeutic and social work support to help families resolve those issues. In the intake department, child protective caseworkers are required to confront clients about allegations of abuse and use their power and persuasion to create desired behaviors. In comparison, at the treatment department child protective caseworkers' roles are of a therapeutic nature and resemble more of the standard social worker role. They are expected to express empathy towards the situation that led to the referral and a helping orientation to their clients. We should expect, then, that caseworkers in different departments manage their own emotions in at least somewhat different ways and for different needs. There has been scant comparison research on the emotional labor stemming from differences in caseworker roles, and even less on the role that humor plays in emotional labor processes.

Knowing how humor comes into play in all this helps us understand the multitude of ways employees and departments deal with stress and negative emotions that appear in their daily work with clients. This also helps leaders understand how they can harness the power of humor and develop positive strategies for its use among their employees and organizations. Thus, this research extends literature about impacts of humor in relation to stress and emotions at the organizational level and has policy implications that can be made.

CHAPTER SUMMARY AND BOOK OVERVIEW

Throughout this chapter, we have reviewed how Office of Children, Youth and Families employees are exposed to situations with a high degree of negative emotions and stressors during employment that revolve around neglect and the physical and sexual abuse of children (Anderson, 2000). The stress and negative emotions that caseworkers experience need to be managed as part of their emotional labor. Humor can be a tool that caseworkers deploy to manage their emotions and the stressors they experience. This qualitative research demonstrates that Office of Children, Youth and Families employees experience gallows humor to manage those negative emotions and stressors.

Understanding how employees individually and as a group manage emotions and stressors can reveal both deficiencies and strengths of both the employee and the organization. This can help leaders make decisions regarding their organization. The purpose of this book was to explore how humor is used within the Office of Children, Youth and Families and what the use of humor, including dark gallows humor, reveals about how employees experience stress and manage their emotions. This includes a focus on understanding both the negative and positive aspects of using humor to manage emotions on the individual, within work groups, and on the organization.

Phoebe and Dani's experience that frigid day in January, displayed the range of negative emotions she experienced from the dilemmas she faced when conducting her fieldwork. They assisted a teen's safety needs, uncovered a methamphetamine manufacturing operation, ensured the mother received care from Emergency Medical Services (EMS), and assisted police as they dealt with their investigation. They did this under the pressure of accusations of planting drugs and resistance from the teenager they were trying to help. To top it off, they did this in subzero temperatures and were locked in the back of a police car during the chaos. This book explores the accounts of many child welfare caseworkers, like Phoebe and Dani. Their stories provide an illustration of the stress and the emotions they experience due to similar dilemmas they encounter at work and how using humor to cope assists them in accomplishing their tasks for better and worse.

Chapter 2

Understanding the Child
Welfare Caseworker

Office of Children, Youth and Families employees are exposed to cases involving a high degree of neglect and physical and sexual abuse of children that cue intense emotional responses in both the caseworker and referred family (Anderson, 2000). They are also tasked with solving the problems of their clients yet have little control over their actions, and who are often frustrated with the allegations against them, making work even more difficult and engendering disappointment from its lack of impact (Howell, 2008). Similarly, caseworkers can be emotionally shocked by the situations and details of abuse (Taris & Schreurs, 2009) leading to anger, depression, uneasiness, guilt, loneliness, and helplessness. Miscommunication and conflict among caseworkers can contribute to job stress and impact employee satisfaction, burnout, and dropout. To deal with this, caseworkers are encouraged to find their own coping mechanisms to reduce stress (Farester, 2016) and depending on how well they cope, the quality of their services potentially suffers (Heverling, 2011).

Coping

Both destructive and productive stress-coping mechanisms are used by employees, sometimes in combination, to address stress and negative emotions related to work duties (Farester, 2016; Heverling, 2011). For instance, one employee may cope through substance abuse (a destructive coping strategy) while also coping through exercise (a productive coping strategy). Heverling's (2011) research reveals that common destructive strategies among child welfare workers include disordered eating, alcohol abuse, and smoking which harm employees and personal relationships and ultimately increase employee burnout. Child welfare employees also use common productive coping mechanisms such as physical activity, communal venting, utilization of relaxation techniques, and communicating (Heverling, 2011).

Child welfare employees require social support and to process traumatic events that they encounter in fulfilling their job duties to be successful (Conrad & Kellar-Guenther, 2006). It is imperative that leaders understand employees and support management processes in the workplace.

Humor constitutes both a coping and bonding tool. Gallows humor, a specific type of dark humor defined by its highlighting of traumatic situations as particularly funny, can be used in the moment of tragedy to bond with others experiencing the situation, manage stress, and suppress intrusive emotion. Previous research has shown humor is a mechanism of social support used by groups to bond after traumatic events (Turcotte, 2017) and a form of control in hopeless situations (Obrdlik, 1942). It can be categorized as a type of trauma coping (Johnson, 2007) because it constitutes "efforts to manage specific external and/or internal demands that are appraised as taxing or exceeding the person's resources" (Folkman, Lazarus, Dunkel-Schetter, DeLongis & Gruen, 1986, p. 993).

Humor provides a lens into organizations as well. We assert that the study of humor within organizations such as the child welfare system can reveal weaknesses in support and gaps in coping, which provide a window of insight for leaders to strategize needed changes. Furthermore, humor—when harnessed as a tool—can help employees manage stressors, reduce negative emotions, attenuate compassion fatigue, protect against secondary trauma, and diminish burnout. Gaining greater insights into these assertions is the aim of this book.

HUMOR IN CHILD WELFARE DILEMMAS

A myriad of problems with differing levels of urgency come from referrals of general neglect, physical abuse, and sexual abuse of children at the Office of Children, Youth and Families. Caseworkers are given tasks that encompass solving problems related to inadequate housing, neglectful supervision, sexual abuse, physical abuse, street crime, drug and alcohol addiction, incorrigibility, truancy, and even death. Child welfare caseworkers perform these tasks under the added stress of working in an environment of high staff turnover (Johnco et al., 2014; Salloum, Kondrat, Johno & Olson, 2015) and low pay (Salloum et al., 2015). Furthermore, they struggle to keep up with training and procedures that are regularly modified according to frequently changing organizational policies and child welfare laws.

Chief among these concerns are monumental caseloads, which are a unique high occupational stressor for child welfare caseworkers (Stalker, Mandell,

Frensch, Harvey & Wright, 2007) that accompany endless amounts of paperwork. Caseworkers interviewed for this research often recalled humorous experiences regarding high caseloads and paperwork. For instance, Gina, an intake caseworker for 25 years stated that humor "is a really, really good way to let out stress because everybody's running around, freaking out about trying to meet deadlines." She went on to mention that there is a "never-ending, never-ever ending gobs of paperwork and you're always scrambling to prioritize what needs done first" and she is "stressed to the max." To cope with these stressors the "only way that you can release that" is through "humor."

"Then Out the Window She Goes"

Much humor also revolves around frustrations encountered during visits to clients' homes, which is accompanied by intensive paperwork even if the client was a "no-show" or noncompliant. For instance, Crystal, an intake caseworker of nearly three years recalled an instance of a noncompliant client that was a "no-show." She was directed by her supervisor to conduct a scheduled visit to a client's apartment on the second floor. To her annoyance, when she got there no one answered the door nor appeared home. As she walked down from the apartment to the car, the stress and negativity began to build in her mind as this meant additional paperwork, rescheduling, and a later return for another visitation. By the time Crystal got to her car she was really frustrated with the situation. She returned to the car to see Julie, her coworker, keeled over laughing. "What!?" Crystal said. Julie then revealed that when Crystal was knocking on the door, the client opened and climbed out of the second-floor apartment window, in her underwear, and jumped into the bushes. She then scurried to the neighbor's apartment to hide. Crystal burst into laughter as well. After a few minutes, they calmed down enough to call into the office to figure out how to handle the situation.

The situation that Crystal and Julie experienced is a great example of how humor diffuses stress. In stark terms, Crystal's situation intensified. It went from frustration about noncompliance to the potential of criminal fleeing. Rather than her feelings of frustration also intensifying from this dilemma, she and Julie turned the situation into something humorous and then used the momentary break to recover and take the next steps to address the dilemmas from the noncompliant client.

COUNTING FEW WINS

Beyond noncompliance, it's difficult for both intake and treatment caseworkers to "count the wins" with their clients. Organizationally, intake caseworkers, who investigate allegations, rarely see any outcomes related to the family's progress due to their role. They only work with the family for a short period during investigations and do not see what occurs to the family on a long-term basis. If they do meet the family again, it is usually due to another investigation open on the family. Therefore, intake caseworkers typically never see any case "wins."

On the other hand, treatment caseworkers assist families to resolve situations about the safety concerns of children. They work with the family to alleviate the concerns and have a higher likelihood of seeing a family succeed. However, they too see few "wins." Their caseloads sometimes consist of families they have worked with for years who continue to struggle with the same issues. Likewise, families that remain on their caseload and are not able to meet their goals and are most likely active through the court system, which usually results in the removal of a child(ren) from their birth home. For those families that can meet the requirements of treatment, the caseworkers close their case and, thus, do not know the long-term outcome of those families that do not return to the agency. Therefore, they are unable to see the fruits of their labor and gain the positive emotions associated with learning the long-term progress of a family. For the families they do hear from again, it is due to another referral that was made on the family.

Child welfare caseworkers, in general, frequently see and experience more negative outcomes than positive. Trish, an intake caseworker for two to three years and a treatment caseworker for one year, called this absurdity akin to "living in the movie Groundhog Day." But if this is so, why do they stay at the organization? Why do they persist? Perhaps philosophers Albert Camus and Thomas Nagel can shed some light into these questions.

WHY CHILD WELFARE CASEWORKERS PERSIST

Philosophers Albert Camus (1990) and Thomas Nagel (1971) both theorize about absurdity of lasting meaning and purpose in human action, which is known as existentialist philosophy. Camus refers to this absurdity as stemming from the contrast of individuals' desire to create lasting meaning within the universe and the reality that they are mere, weak, and temporary specks of dust with consciousness. Camus's philosophical writings grapple with questions around a reality that cannot maintain our expectations for meaning. Ultimately, he concludes that humans must take a heroic approach to this contradiction by continuing to strive for meaning regardless of the unimportant impact may have in the grand scheme of the universe (Maden, 2020).

Thomas Nagel similarly focuses on absurdity of the human condition due to how serious we view ourselves in relation to our ability to take a broader perspective of the world (Maden, 2020). His focus is on the inward conflict of engaging in the absurdness of life even though we recognize the randomness—and ultimately meaninglessness—of what we do.

Whereas Camus (1944) suggests that humans take a defiant stance—like Sisyphus—through a continued attempt to heroically press forward to live for meaning, Nagel (1971) argues that this approach does not address the unimportance of the situation itself. Therefore, he recommends that individuals approach absurdity *ironically* rather than *heroically* (Maden, 2020). Nagel (1971) encourages us to approach the absurdness in life as comical and have a laugh about it (Maden, 2020).

In relation to child welfare caseworkers, since humans desire meaning and purpose in their lives, humor can bridge the gap between expectations of work for "wins" that reveal a greater purpose and the reality of high stress and limited results. Caseworkers have the goal of improving the lives of others. These expectations are most often met by the sobering fact that many, if not most, clients will continue to struggle with the same issues, making little progress after an intervention. Caseworkers continue to be met by these losses. This begs the previous question: why do they persist and what does humor have to do with this? According to Nagel's humor in the absurd theory, even though child welfare caseworkers will have the reality that they will see clients fail they can still have a desire to fulfill their meaning of helping others to live as the best versions of themselves. To do so, they can use humor to deal with the irony of their futile attempts at impacting the larger world.

RELEVANT THEORIES OF HUMOR

Setting the existentialist philosophy of Nagel and Camus aside, a background of the theory of humor, aspects of the stress process model, and the sociology of emotions was needed to understand the research questions for this study. Humor research, across disciplines, typically classifies its use into three categories; superiority, incongruity, and relief theory (Morreall 1983; 1987). Research on humor in the discipline of social science has focused on functionalist, conflict, symbolic interactionist, phenomenological approach, and comparative-historical approach (Kuipers, 2008). There have also been overall themes in the study of humor including (1) "humor [at] the expense of others and more generally the "dark side of humor," (2) "the relation between humor and laughter," and (3) "the study of humorous forms and genres, including mediatized forms of humor" (Kuipers, 2008, p. 386). Although humor in the United States is used in a variety of ways and serves a few purposes, for this study we focused on how humor is a coping mechanism that aids in decreasing stress (Johnson, 2007) and regulates other emotions.

Stressors can be random or systemic, and organizational stress can result in job strain. The demand-control-support model reviews that there are coping strategies, such as social supports and control (Thoits, 1995) that can address stressors. Even though studies associated with the model are typically quantitative, this still sheds light on the importance of interpersonal social support processes. Furthermore, the theoretical context of this book includes a foundation of the sociology of emotions that reveals how emotions are managed to decrease stress and regulate conflicting emotions. An area of the sociology of emotions reviewed in this book is emotional labor, which is "the process by which workers are expected to manage their feelings in accordance with organizationally defined rules and guidelines" (Wharton, 2009, p. 147). There are also subareas of humor theory, stress theory, and the sociology of emotions that demonstrate the importance of social relationships. Therefore, those areas are also included in this book. In summary, a theoretical understanding of the theory of humor, the stress process model, and the sociology of emotions was needed, to better research the questions in this study.

Chapter 3

Why So Funny?

What makes you laugh? Humor seems like such a simple and familiar word to most of us. A majority of us have had exposure to humor but also have our own idea of what is funny. Media exposes us to stand-up comedians, such as Chris Rock, Gary Own, Kevin Hart, and Amy Schumer to name a few. We are also exposed to comedic genre films and television shows where actors like Melissa McCarthy, Tyler Perry, Steve Carell, and Jim Carry make us laugh. Social media, television, radio broadcasting, streaming platforms, and in-person theater venues all provide a platform for humor and comedic personalities as well, such as David Dobrik, Bobbi Althoff, and Khaby Lame. As you think about comedy that makes you laugh (and doesn't), you'll see that it illustrates that individuals prefer different things that are funny. This preference can be due to the types of jokes, their content, and/or their style of delivery. It also has a lot to do with who you are and your background as an audience member which will profoundly impact what is humorous and what makes you laugh. Some people find jokes about everyday struggles hilarious, while others do not. Some people enjoy slapstick and physical comedy, while others do not. Why is this? What makes us find something funny? Even though it's not funny to study, some social science researchers have paid attention to the meaning and dynamics of humor. This chapter reviews aspects of humor research, in order to understand why we enjoy humor and why what is considered funny can differ greatly from person to person.

HUMOR IN SOCIAL THEORY

Rather than being addressed in a stand-alone theory, humor as a social interaction has been incorporated into various social theories that explain its social purpose. Additionally, it is only marginally incorporated into theories within the social science disciplines leaving the understanding of humor's purpose in each only partially treated. Social theorists have largely defined humor as an act of communication that is perceived as humorous (Vivona, 2013) and noted that much of humor is dependent on specific norms and cultural contexts of the time and place it is used in (Kuipers, 2008). Below we review some of the various ways that major social theories have tried to make sense of humor.

Functionalism

One attempt to understand humor as a social phenomenon is through the theory of functionalism. Functionalism focuses on aspects of humor as a social function in a society or within groups, and to maintain social order (Kuipers, 2008). Superiority, Incongruity, and Relief theories address humor through the functionalist approach (Morreall 1983; 1987). Superiority theory identifies humor as a cultural safety function for dehumanizing classes and categories of people in ways that reinforce stratification and inequality. For instance, Coser's (1960) research noted that laughter used by those in power maintains a sense of social order and hierarchy. This largely focuses on the function of humor made by and for powerful groups at the expense of the less powerful (Vogler, 2011). Incongruity theories of humor refer to humor that extends from when individuals encounter contexts and events that differ from their socially predicted outcomes. Here humor is especially functional for reinforcing social norms and normative contexts (Kuipers, 2008). In this functionalist sense, humor is a form of social control (Billig 2005). Relief theory, which is derived from Sigmund Freud's *Jokes and their Relation to the Unconscious* (1976), refers to the value of humor as the relieving feelings that come from making others laugh. Similarly, Dundes (1987) argues that the use of dark humor can be used by individuals to distance oneself from traumatic events and continue as normal. Taken together, these three theories that extend from functionalism—Superiority, Incongruity, and Relief—have value in understanding the social and organizational benefits and cost of the use of humor are in its ability to help organizations remain functional.

Conflict Theory

Conflict theorists have focused on humor, examining its role in reproducing social conflict (Speier 1998). For instance, Obrdlik (1942) demonstrated how the use of humor among the population of Czechoslovakia while under Nazi control during WWII boosted citizen morale and strengthened resistance efforts. His work illustrated how humor can assist group solidarity among oppressed groups and be an alternative form of relief when expressions of anger or outward resistance are prohibited and dangerous. He said that the jokes told among the citizens "bolsters the resistance of the victims and, at the same time, it undermines the morale of the oppressors" (p. 713). The conflict approach also focuses on offensive humor often directed toward minorities, and such xenophobic/racist, sexist, and homophobic forms of political humor can be used to drive wedges, enflame conflict, and dehumanize others (Lockyer and Pickering, 2005).

Symbolic Interactionist

The symbolic interactionist approach to the study of humor illuminates how it helps to create meaning in social interactions (Kuipers, 2008). For instance, Emerson's (1969) work focused on how individuals used humor to create a sense of safety in interactions so that taboo topics could be discussed. Similarly, Goffman (1974) focused on humor as a way of *framing* topics or situations at hand to make them less serious than what would be culturally expected. The symbolic interactionists approach to humor also accounts for the various interactants in the situation including the joker, target, and audience in examining how humor is used to delimit boundaries of groups (Kuipers, 2008). Group culture provides "social solidarity in the functionalist sense" and uses "ingroup humor, repeat jokes, and specific humorous styles and tastes that literally get to define a group, and be used to demarcate its identity" (Kuipers, 2008, p. 379).

Phenomenological Theory

The phenomenological theory views humor as a psychological *outlook* for interpreting aspects of the social world (Kuipers, 2008). This approach typically assesses the differences in the humorous and serious sides of experience and perception. In his book, *Reality in a Looking Glass,* Zijderveld (1982) theorizes how humor provides a unique *looking-glass* view of the world around us, distorting our view of reality and ourselves. The research of Zijderveld (1982), Davis (1993), and Mulkay (1988) all contribute to the phenomenological understanding of humor by examining why people choose to use humor rather than simply share experience openly with others (as cited in Kuipers, 2008).

Despite a diverse number of social science theories that explore the use of humor, there are overarching themes. This includes humor (1) serving as a functional tool for groups and organizations, (2) creating solidarities and divisions between groups of people, and (3) impacting how individuals see the self, others, and social contexts. For our study, we employ all three insights to understand Office of Children, Youth and Families employees and the forms of humor occurring among them.

THE DOUBLE-EDGE SWORD OF HUMOR

Gallows humor or humor amid death and suffering (Obrdlik, 1942; Vivona, 2013) is also known as dark or black humor, which is identified by its grim and morbid subject matter and focus on irreverence for matters that typically evoke emotions of sadness or fear (Coughlin, 2002). Gallows humor is sometimes used as a coping strategy by social workers, journalists, police officers, soldiers, crime scene investigators, and among employees that work with sexual exploitation of children (Buchanan & Keats, 2011; Riolli & Savicki, 2010; Roth & Vivona, 2010; van Wormer & Boes, 1997; Wright, Powell & Ridge, 2006). For instance, Watson's (2011) research notes that gallows humor can reduce grief and frustration among healthcare providers when used away from the client they serve. Howell's (2008) research on Florida child protective investigators showed how they used humor in the field to distance themselves from situations, suppress emotions they were feeling and aid in completing their tasks. Research also shows that humor relieves stress (Wright et al., 2006) and normalizes difficult situations (Alvarado, 2013; Francis, 1994). Yet research is mixed on the effectiveness of humor on reducing stress, such as Coughlin's (2002) study on police officers that found no correlation between gallows humor and lower stress levels.

Service employees report that dark humor can help them cope with the traumas of the job (Craun & Bourke, 2015). The act of making others laugh in difficult situations provides a socially appropriate outlet for the release of negative emotions (Vivona, 2013) and an avenue to express reserved concern (Altenau, 2010). Professionals using gallows humor to talk about the morbid, grotesque, and unnerving situations encountered in these difficult careers can also help remove the social constraints associated with taboo topics (Monro, 1988). For instance, Meerlo's (1966) research among military personnel during wartime illustrated how joking and laughter was used to distance oneself from the fears of battlefield dangers and prevented desertion in the face of danger. This may only be temporary relief, but it likely helps to prevent burnout in contexts of uncertainty and in dangerous situations (Monro, 1988; Scott, 2007).

An aspect of gallows and dark humor that we pay careful attention to is that the act of making light of the suffering of others can turn into a type of victim blaming (Atkinson, 2006; Rowe & Regehr, 2010). When it is used for this function, it links us back to the ideas about humor in both superiority theory and conflict theory (Gruner, 1978; Billig, 2005). Simply put, dark humor can reinforce feelings of superiority an individual has over others or other groups.

Gallows humor can also be viewed as offensive and insensitive and thus inappropriate in the modern workplace (Coughlin, 2002). Humor like this is sometimes seen as targeting others, aggressive, and threatening and therefore, can negatively impact work culture (Kuipers, 2008). Gallows humor at the expense of a victim can be viewed as a signal that an employee lacks compassion and cannot perform quality work (Craun & Bourke, 2014). In human services, use of this type of humor may have the unintended consequence of contributing to victim blaming service recipients for the situation they are in and lead to the degradation of the services they need (Rowe & Regehr, 2010).

Humor can provide insight into divisions among groups (Ferguson & Ford, 2008) within the workplace as well as in the public and among other entities (Regehr & Bober, 2005). Child protective caseworkers can feel a sense of belonging or isolation with their coworkers. The use of dark humor can be a signal of solidarity and insider status and have an impact on employee self-esteem (Rowe & Regehr, 2010). However, humor in groups may have negative ramifications due to its effects of decreasing the likelihood that some individuals will openly share their feelings (Rowe & Regehr, 2010). Regehr, Goldberg, and Hughes's (2002) research on paramedics supports this idea when they found that black humor concealed underlying emotions. Some individuals feared expressing emotions due to society's view of those emotions being non- masculine. Using humor further suppressed those individuals from wanting to express their emotions.

As reviewed above, there is a dearth of research directly examining gallows humor among child protective caseworkers, yet we already know a lot about analogous careers associated with traumatic situation (Johnson, 2007) where the use of humor to cope is common (Craun & Bourke, 2015).

An understanding of the theory of humor provides a better foundation to learn more about the types of humor that Office of Children, Youth and Families employees utilize and their consequences. Likewise, the review of research on gallows humor can aid in understanding of the negative and positive impacts of using this form of humor more generally. As we will see in future chapters, we apply this understanding to assess humor of intake and treatment employees in the child welfare setting.

Likewise, the use of humor can provide organizational leaders with insights about how employees are managing the normalization of their job duties, as well as the culture of their organization. A closer look at what makes employees laugh and the jokes they tell can give insight into what is bothering them individually and as a group. This can also shed light on the strengths and weaknesses within organizational culture, structure, and processes.

A TRAGEDY TURNED TO COMEDY

Jewel, an intake, treatment, and general caseworker for over 12 years, recalls creating a joke referring to the unpleasant appearance of one specific client, a mother struggling with drug abuse and having trouble properly caring for her children who revealed to caseworkers that she was pregnant. Prior to sharing the joke told among her coworkers, Jewel expressed extreme frustration that this client's young children were continually being referred back into the child welfare system again and again. Anticipating another child this client would add to the referral load, she stated, "How stupid can one be if you don't have your own child now, why would you bring another child into this world and think that you're going to keep this child [out of the system]."

Jewel talked at length about her annoyance with the persistence of the drug abuse problems of the mother, which were identified as the major contributing factor to the referrals. The client's addiction had become so overwhelming that she was regularly neglectful of her children. Jewel felt powerless after multiple attempts to help the client with treatment and recovery. She saw her deteriorate over the years and watched hopelessly as the children suffered from cycles of neglect and removals.

When Jewel learned that the mother had become pregnant again, her coworkers and she created jokes about the client's unattractiveness and sexual appeal which were embedded with their frustration. Jewel reported that the client weighed around seventy-five pounds, smelled bad, was disheveled and "looked like a drug user with terrible teeth." Jewel and her coworker joked with each other by incredulously wondering how any man would desire sex with this client. Jewel said she would joke about this with her coworkers by feigning jealously that "she gets more men than me."

Jewel also joked with her coworkers about the client's drug addiction. She recalls joking about how she would regularly give unconvincing and poor excuses for failing drug tests. Jewel would laugh with coworkers when she would retell stories of the client giving unbelievable accounts after failing a test such as shrugging her shoulders and stating that "she never uses [the drugs]" or eliciting a surprise reaction that "she didn't know how they got into her system." Jewel said, in general, that the jokes about this particularly difficult client "didn't necessarily lift my spirits" but that it provided her with a "mental escape." For Jewel, joking about her client helped her reframe the perpetual failure for her client as comedy rather than tragedy to change the outlook and provided her an outlet of stress relief. Jewel's humor about this client was "basically one thing that got me through it." Jewel used humor as a way of managing the negative emotions she felt and her stress from her client's inability to turn her drug use around for the sake of her children.

Jewel admitted that joking about her client's appearance "made me feel better somehow."

Even though joking helped Jewel find relief in dealing with a particularly difficult case and aided in her ability to keep working, there is an immediate concern that it toes the line (if not crosses it altogether) of professionalism and ethics. It also illustrates what type of stressful conditions caseworkers regularly encounter and the complexity of the problems they face. The use of humor challenges the simple conclusion that the joking from Jewel and her coworkers is just evidence they are a bunch of "bad apples." We feel it focuses us on questions of occupational stress, and especially questions about how people respond when organizations fail to create appropriate outlets for stress to be relieved.

Stress

We focus on two definitions of stress and its relation to work environments to frame our research, which are both closely related to what is known as the "stress-process model." First are external factors in the environment that cause stress, which are known as stressors. In relation to stressors, Thoits (1995, p. 54) defines stress as "any environmental, social, or internal demand, which requires the individual to readjust his/her usual behavior patterns." Complementary to this externally focused definition of stress, Mirowsky and Ross (2003, p. 23) use the term "distress" to describe an internal "unpleasant subjective state" that results from stress. Thoits (1995) shows that as individuals experience stressors, they can become overloaded with stress and exhaust their psychological and/or physical resources resulting in the experience of distress. In this line, "stress" is an umbrella term which describes the general reaction to environmental factors called "stressors," which can ultimately result in "distress" (Mirowsky & Ross, 2003). See figure for a simplistic illustration.

Understanding the relationship between stressors, stress, and distress and knowing about the layers of social and personal risk and protective factors that either exacerbate or mitigate stress is useful in parsing caseworkers' experience of their job and the potential role humor plays in this process.

Sociological theories on stress focus on three common types of stressors: life events, daily hassles, and chronic strains (Thoits, 1995). Life changes have a psychological impact that is a result of the "conditions that produce the events and follow from them" and are "an active and instrumental response to the events, rather than a passive and fatalistic one" (Mirowsky & Ross, 2003, p. 13). Research suggests that undesirable events are stressors (Mirowsky & Ross, 2003; Vinokur & Selzer, 1975). Daily hassles are frequent daily occurrences that may be irritating, such as waiting in traffic. Those with distress

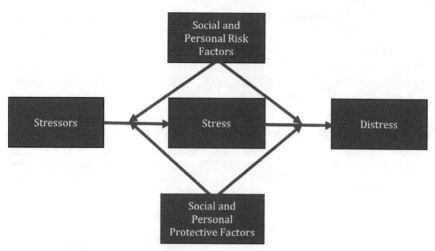

Figure 3.1.   A simplified illustration of stress process.

due to other factors (social factors) are more sensitive to the cause of daily hassles (Mirowsky & Ross, 2003). Daily hassles and life events sometimes do not bring attention to the social causes of stress (Mirowsky & Ross, 2003). Chronic strain refers to stressors that are endured over a long period of time (Mirowsky & Ross, 2003; Farester, 2016) and Office of Children, Youth and Families employees can experience this type of strain. Thus, coping strategies are required to buffer the effects of stress (Thoits, 1995).

Organizational stress on employees results from stressors in the organizational environment (Cooper & Dewe, 2004, Farester, 2016; Lazarus, 1999). Often called "job strain," it is important to understand that employees have different sources of stressors and corresponding levels of stress. This is important to acknowledge for this study because we assume that intake and treatment workers have different stressors, stress, and distress levels—and respond to these factors with different forms of humor. Studying how different Office of Children, Youth and Families caseworkers utilize humor may shed light on what the stressors are as well as what is lacking in coping with stress.

Using the stress-process model framework, we argue that gallows humor is a coping strategy used to mitigate distress (Johnson, 2007) by creating a perception of control and support for caseworkers. Stress theory highlights the importance of protective factors on decreasing stress (Thoits, 1995). Understanding aspects of the stress process model and applying it to humor theory aids in a better understanding of how Office of Children, Youth and Families employees experience stress, what their coping strategies are, and how employees are managing the normalization of their job duties through the use of humor. However, there also needs to be an understanding of the sociology of emotions, which aids in understanding the research questions in this study.

SOCIOLOGY OF EMOTIONS

Over the course of the first author's employment in child welfare, Dr. Landram regularly experienced negative emotions such as frustration, anger, sadness, and despair. However, she rarely felt it appropriate to display these emotions openly. So, for the most part, at work, negative emotions were channeled through humor. The darker the better.

This section reviews the sociology of emotions to understand how people transform emotions in the workplace and the implications of this unrecognized form of labor. We mainly focus interactionists theories that highlight sociocultural factors that contribute to emotions and emotion management (Thoits, 1989). Hochschild (1979) refers to the term emotion management as the readjusting of feelings and expressions of emotions to the demands of the social context. Emotion management is required in private contexts as well as during employment—but typically is distinguished by sociologists referring to the former as emotion management and the latter as emotional labor (despite both sounding like they are organizationally situated). The emotion management perspective includes the examination of emotion vocabularies, emotional beliefs, feeling rules, and the variety of cognitive, bodily, interpersonal, and cultural tools that individuals create and use to conform their emotions to the expectations of the context (Hochschild, 1979).

Feeling rules can be universal or belong to a social group (Hochschild, 1979) and have varying expectations for gender (Fields, Copp & Kleinman, 2006). For example, feeling rules in western culture suggest that women should display more caring emotions, while men are permitted to express anger more openly (Hochschild, 1979).

Emotional management feeling and display rules are omnipresent—formal and informal—in modern work organizations. Child protective caseworkers experience emotions throughout their employment and are expected to manage those emotions. Office of Children, Youth and Families employees consist of caseworkers, supervisors, administration, independent living workers, lawyers, paralegals, foster care workers, clerical units, and fiscal departments. These employees work with judges, detectives, police officers, defense attorneys, child attorneys, service providers, adoptive parents, community members, biological parents, foster families, and children. Each of these entities has its own demands for the employee and expectations of how they should manage their emotions. In addition, employees have their own job description and laws that they must follow. This leads to multiple expectations and conflicts in aligning emotions with the demands placed on them.

Office of Children, Youth and Families caseworkers can also experience conflicting emotions due to varied family contexts they experience. It's a normalized part of the job to regularly encounter contexts of child sexual abuse, interpersonal family violence, and child neglect as part of the job. As child protective caseworkers experience emotions related to each case they are working with, personal emotion management and professional emotional labor is required. It is no wonder caseworker employees can become emotionally exhausted from these interactions, which can affect their work performance (Taris & Schreurs, 2009). Employees that work in emotionally demanding circumstances can experience burnout and compassion fatigue (West, 2015).

Understanding feeling rules, display rules, framing rules, situational factors, and emotional management helps to form a better understanding of how Office of Children, Youth and Families employees experience emotions and how utilizing humor may be a strategy for managing those emotions and distress. Craun and Bourke's (2014) research on Internet Crimes Against Children Task Force personnel demonstrated how employees use humor and gallows humor to address their overall well-being. Likewise, Pogrebin and Poole's (1988) research noted that law enforcement employees use humor to build rapport with one another and this increased the cohesion of their groups. The use of humor can also aid organizational leaders in understanding their organization's culture and norms, how employees are dealing with stress and what issues they need to address.

Intake and Treatment Caseworkers

Hochschild's (2003) book, *The Managed Heart,* assesses emotional labor among bill collectors and flight attendants. Although both experience emotional labor and utilize the same processes to regulate emotional rules, the flight attendants enhance the status of their customers while bill collectors diminish this status. Child protective caseworkers' tasks consist of determining abuse and therapeutic aspects of helping families resolve those issues. Some Office of Children, Youth and Families agencies have separate departments for these tasks: the intake department (investigators) and the treatment department (those that help families resolve issues). However, some agencies only have general child protective caseworkers that perform both functions. Does this create conflict for the general employees when their roles change? It may, but for this research, we mainly focus on caseworkers in the intake and treatment departments since most organizations operate in this manner and we are interested in assessing group dynamics, between the two departments and individuals within each department and how they use humor to manage emotions and stress. However, assessing general child protective caseworker's emotional work and use of humor may be an area for future research.

Even though the Office of Children, Youth and Families have the same mission and expectations for their employees, each job-related task and department experiences emotions differently and therefore may manage other's emotions differently. The intake department child protective caseworkers are required to confront clients about allegations of abuse and use their authority to create desired behaviors. This can require employees to suppress their own emotions to perform job tasks. In return, they utilize gallows humor as a form of emotional management. Office of Children, Youth and Families intake child protective caseworkers suppress similar emotions while evoking others through gallows humor. The treatment department child protective caseworker role is of a therapeutic nature and resembles more of the standard social worker role. They can express more feelings of empathy and therefore may manage their emotions and experience gallows humor differently. This led to the question; does the treatment department child protective caseworkers manage their emotions and use humor in the same way?

The Office of children, Youth and Families have the same standards for how both departments should be managing emotions and stress, as well as how caseworkers should be representing themselves and their cases to others. Hochschild's (2003) found that training was different among flight attendants and bill collectors due to their employee role and how this played a part in emotional management. This research suggests that there needs to be training and education about the differences and similarities in emotions, stress, and humor among the two departments. Training that prepares an employee for their particular role and how they may experience emotions and the emotions of others is needed. It is also important to understand when humor is a helpful function and when it is not, as well as what that tells researchers and organizational leaders about the organization and their employees.

SUMMARY

Child welfare caseworkers like Phoebe, Crystal, and Jewel, as well as the other participants in this study reveal how humor, stress, and emotions are experienced in the child welfare system. Furthermore, research about humor, stress, and emotions helps understand the role of these topics within the child welfare system. As we have discussed in some of these case examples, humor can present itself in the back of a police car (like Phoebe experienced), at the realization that your client would rather climb out of a window than meet with you (like Crystal experienced), or a caseworker may find themselves laughing at the appearance of their client (like Jewel).

Our findings on the high frequency of the use of humor and the fact that caseworkers report they are unable to do the job without using humor reveal that humor is a major part of the lives of child welfare caseworkers. Rather it is for addressing the absurd or dilemmas associated with stress and negative emotions. Many participants in this research noted how humor is essential to decrease "burnout" and "turnover." During an interview with Mandy (intake caseworker for five and a half years and a treatment caseworker for six months) she explained that humor is essential "it's just the culture, the way of the world, the way of that world." Humor is essential to decrease "burnout" and "turnover." Jewel, who has been an intake, treatment, and general case-worker for over 12 years, expressed that humor is part of the job because they "deal with some dark and deep stuff. If you can't laugh about it, your mental health is going to be compromised." She went on to explain that humor provides her "relief" and for those that do not use humor or say anything negative it is not realistic because "no one can live by that"; "not in this field."

All the information in this chapter and the previous chapters provide a better understanding of how humor and gallows humor are experienced among Office of Children, Youth and Families employees, what the negative and positive impacts of the use of gallows humor are and the similarities and differences of the utilization of gallows humor among employees. Figure 3 provides a concept map overview of the literature discussed in the above chapters and how it relates to the Office of Children, Youth and Families.

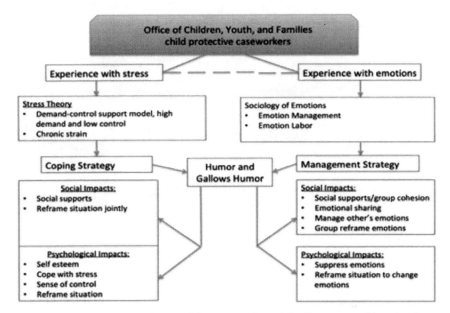

Figure 3.2.   Concept map that provides an overview of the literature and how it relates to the Office of Children, Youth and Families.

Chapter 4

What's So Funny?

Phoebe, Crystal, and Jewel's stories are just a few examples of the many caseworkers interviewed that use humor to lessen the jolt of the cobblestones on their road to helping others. This chapter, chapter 5, and chapter 6, review accounts of other caseworkers that have similar experiences. As we have noted, child welfare caseworkers experience situations and dilemmas in the course of their work which produces stress and negative emotions that they are required to cope with and manage.

As a reminder, our research seeks to understand how both humor and gallows humor are experienced among Office of Children, Youth and Families employees, what the negative and positive impacts of the use of these types of humor are and assess the similarities and differences of the utilization of humor among different types of caseworkers. Our specific research questions that guided this book are as follows: 1) How do Office of Children, Youth and Families employees (intake and treatment) experience humor and gallows humor, and what does that reveal about how they are managing stress and emotions related to their employment? 2) What are the negative and positive effects of the use of gallows humor among individuals, groups, and the organization? 3) Are there any similarities and/or differences in how intake and treatment employees utilize gallows humor?

Our approach to answering these research questions is through analysis of humor used to manage these dilemmas in social work. This chapter delves deeper into exploring these questions in three ways. In the first section, we review the varied types of caseworker humor including pranks, games, nonverbal humor, deadpanning humor, and humorous internal dialogue. Discussing this allows for an accounting of the various ways humor occurs within the Office of Children, Youth and Families. In the second section, we discuss the context in which humor is used. The circumstances that warrant humor include discussion of high caseloads and copious paperwork, in reliving case situations where a caseworker loses control, in retelling stories of troubling client behaviors, high emotions situations, and less-than-ideal working conditions. This provides a deeper understanding of how caseworkers are utilizing humor to cope with stress and manage emotions due to the dilemmas they encounter. The first two sections answer the first research question: How do Office of Children, Youth and Families employees (intake and treatment) experience humor and gallows humor, and what does that reveal about how they are managing stress and emotions related to their employment?

In the third section of this chapter, we analyze the impacts of humor in this context. Here we focus our attention on the individual positive outcomes of humor for caseworkers including relief from stress and negative emotions. We show how this is a method to brush off negative emotions created by the regular stressful dilemmas they experience. We also examine the negative effects of the use of humor (at the microlevel), which includes the masking of traumas that child welfare caseworkers experience, the alteration of their personal identity, and disruption of connections with family and friends not employed in the profession. This discussion answers the first part of our second research question: What are the negative and positive effects of the use of gallows humor among individuals, groups, and the organization?

STRATEGIES FOR UTILIZING HUMOR

Child welfare caseworkers utilize different strategies to express their humor in the office. This most often involves office pranks and meme humor. Each type of humor is intended to build social solidarity among caseworkers by signaling common backstage knowledge and familiarity with the work. Although most humor of this type is either allowed or encouraged by managers and received positively by coworkers, sometimes it spills over into being considered inappropriate by each group. Even in very few instances, caseworkers reported that this type of humor was harmful.

OFFICE PRANK HUMOR AND COLLEGIAL BONDING

Pranks and funny games generally have a positive impact. This type of humor allows caseworkers to be a part of a team and binds them together. It is also a type of preparatory emotion work that prepares them for the emotions and stress they may encounter in the field. Even though humor can build these bonds and is a method of preparatory work, it does require an established trust and denotes an in-group status.

Peter (intake caseworker, 3 years) recalled a time that one of his coworkers secretly "taped his phone" down in a way that the switch hook didn't release. Peter spent several hours that day perplexed by not being able to answer his ringing phone. When he finally discovered the prank, he was angry and sought revenge on the person that did this to him. When he learned it was one of his friends at work, whom he trusted, and that the prank was intended to lighten his mood. Rose, an intake caseworker for 16 years and a general caseworker for 3 years, also said that her agency coworkers pranked each other by taping down the receiver hooks of other caseworker's phones. She stated that coworkers did this to make the day lighter. It is a method to help her cope as well as assist others with coping with "the challenges" and "difficult[ies] of the job."

Caseworkers also mentioned other types of pranks that occur in the child welfare culture. In Olivia's office, there was a bathing suit that kept mysteriously being placed on caseworker's chairs. It is a "huge like tankini" that "keeps ending up on people's chairs like the back of their chairs." She remembers coming to work one day and it was on the back of her chair. Olivia (treatment caseworker for 5 years) reports that it was "something that makes everyone laugh because it's just like this random bathing suit ends up on your seat." She thinks that this humor "boosts morale." She never discovered who put it on her chair, but she knew the torch had to be passed on. Once the prank was played on her it was then her unspoken job to pass the bathing suit on to the next person. These actions reinforced bonding and inner group status.

Jade, a general caseworker for 6 years, expressed that she is "grateful" that her office would "pull pranks on one another." She stated that there need to be moments involving humor to break up the seriousness of the day. A coworker at her office is "terrified of garden gnomes." Another time Jade and her coworkers hid "garden gnomes throughout the office" to make everyone laugh. This was also a form of morale, whether they noticed it or not at the time. Garden gnomes were not the only source of pranks they used. Around the Halloween season a scary movie called Helene came out. Her coworker replaced everyone's personal pictures with "creepy grandma aunt Helene" from the movie. The whole office was confused and kept wondering who was changing pictures. Therefore, an internal investigation went on related to this. Jade recalls it was like the game Clue, "like, it was, you know, the paralegal Mandy in the kitchen with you know, the Xerox printer." She stated that the pictures being replaced were so funny, but then the internal investigation Clue-style game topped it and made it hilarious. For Jade, this type of humor kept her "going because you realize like, yeah, it's serious, but you need to laugh to keep, you know, yourself and checking your emotions in check, and know that you're still a person at the end of the day."

Violet's (intake caseworker for 5 years and treatment caseworker for 1 year) office also liked to play pranks on one another to break up the intensity of the job. Caseworkers in her office liked turning the music up really loud before they parked the company car for the day. This way once another caseworker would get into the car they were scared and overwhelmed by loud music. She thinks that pranks like this "helps" them "just move forward" and "feel better."

Interestingly, lots of pranking at different offices involved the use of dolls. Sabrina, an intake caseworker for 2 years, said that she and her coworkers enjoyed pulling pranks with a doll that they brought to the office. First, she and her coworkers at the office found a scary face online that they printed, cut out, and attached to the baby doll. They also added a knife to the doll that made it look menacing. Then they gave it the name, "Dolly." As a prank, they would then move Dolly "from desk to desk" when coworkers weren't paying attention. Eventually, the doll became the de facto prank to play on new employees. Sabrina and her team of pranksters would put it on a new coworker's desk and then wait in anticipation for the moment that they would discover the doll. The caseworkers would then laugh at the reaction of surprise of their new coworker.

This long running prank continued until Dolly went missing. Even in the absence of the doll, the fun with it at the office continued. When Sabrina and her coworker Mandy couldn't find Dolly, they did what any seasoned investigator would do. They designed and printed a "missing child" poster for her and hung it up in the office. Mandy and Sabrina acknowledged that these pranks were "super childish humor." However, they also mentioned this type of pranking humor brought her coworkers together, quickly broke the ice with new employees, and provided distraction that helped manage the stressors at work. Sabrina rationalized the pranking by stating that the "job is just so difficult" that she and her coworkers had to find "humor in it somewhere."

At a separate office, Kelly (an intake caseworker for 5 years and a treatment caseworker for 3 years) and her coworkers also played pranks with dolls on one another. Her office had a surplus of anatomically correct dolls. In the past, these dolls were widely used in the forensic interview process as a tool for victim children to relay the sexual or physical abuse that occurred to them. However, Kelly's child welfare agency had moved away from utilizing these dolls during interviews. At Kelly's office, the administration decided not to immediately discard the unused anatomically correct dolls. Instead, they were stored in the office. Caseworkers began using the dolls to prank each other by placing the dolls in various areas of the office in inappropriate positions. The dolls were most often positioned in a lude manner at a caseworker's desk with the intention that they would be surprised by its discovery. Kelly recalls the pranks being widely shared among coworkers and that they continued with the pranks until their administration finally decided to dispose of the dolls.

Surprisingly, other caseworkers at different locations in this study also used dolls as a source of pranking humor. Phoebe (intake caseworker for 9 years and treatment caseworker for 1 year) and her coworkers enjoyed playing pranks on each other involving anatomically correct dolls. Her office also stopped using those dolls for interviews, and as a result they had some dolls in their office. For fun, caseworkers would put the dolls in each other's offices in "funny poses." These positions consisted of "all kinds of weird sexual like positions." Phoebe reported that these types of pranks occurred all the time "because it was funny" and "probably to help" with the "hard" and "serious" work they do. She went on to mention that it brings "a little bit of light to . . . your day."

Child welfare caseworkers also engage in humorous simple games. Ella's (intake caseworker for 2½ years) described a game called "airmail." Her office had cubicles and her coworkers liked to yell "airmail" before they would throw paperwork over the wall onto a coworker's desk. She said that this type of "surprise" humor "breaks the tension." She and her coworkers played the "airmail game" because sometimes there just needed to be a "change" in "the whole atmosphere." This was especially true for times when the office morale was down, people were "getting grumpy" and were "tired because" because they "all put in, like 12-hour, 14-hour days."

Quinton (intake caseworker for 1 year and treatment caseworker for 6 years), enjoyed pranking his supervisor with his coworkers help. Quinton's described his supervisor's behavior of making a certain "weird kind of stoic face" when delivering bad news which he said his coworkers found to be "the funniest" of faces. Quinton and his coworkers pranked the supervisor by printing "blown up pictures of his face" and "put[ting] it around" the office. This made them laugh together and lightened the mood and the atmosphere.

Prank humor also occurs in the form of childish games. Charlotte, an intake caseworker for 5 years, and her coworkers played games at work to cope with their stress. Her office had several units of caseworkers. Each unit consisted of a supervisor and a few caseworkers. It was not uncommon for units to get similar types of cases. For example, one unit would receive several cases with concerns for parental drug abuse, while another unit would mainly get cases with concerns for sexual abuse. To address the stress and emotions associated with this fact, caseworkers at her office designed and gave the supervisors awards related to case assignments. The sexual abuse unit supervisor got an award for the "sexiest supervisor" and the supervisor of the unit that mainly addressed drug and alcohol abuse cases, received an award for "most drugs." This was a way that Charlotte and her coworkers processed the things they were exposed to. Using this humor also brought them together as a team (a positive impact of humor), which reminded them that these types of situations are not always viewed as typical behaviors or following social norms.

Caseworkers noted that pranks usually caused laughter and lightened the mood of the office. However sometimes it did not. Jewel (intake, treatment, and general caseworker for over 12 years) recalls a time when her coworkers played a prank on an intake intern, and it went wrong. Her coworker was known to be a "jokester." The intern (outsider) was answering phones and taking calls for new referrals. Jewel's coworker (insider) decided to call the intern from his office and "pretended to be someone making a report." Jewel stated that the caseworker made up a fake case scenario of sexual assault of a young child that was so "brutal" the intern was traumatized after taking the report. When the intern brought the report to the team she was visibly upset and stated that the referral was an "old guy . . . he was jumping on the trampoline with a younger boy and he got [sexually] excited." She burst into tears and through her sobbing said to the team that she does not know what to do about it. They immediately told her it was a prank intended to be humorous and lighten things up in the office, but the intern remained upset and showed signs of being less trusting of the caseworkers as a result.

Office Meme Humor and Collective Sharing

Child welfare caseworkers also use nonverbal humor such as memes or comics posted throughout offices. A majority of the time the nonverbal posts are about the role of the social worker. Sabrina recalled her office had funny memes about "being a social worker" as well as "procrastination." Peter's office also had memes and comics about being a social worker. However, sometimes nonverbal humor was about other nonwork-related visuals. For example, Gina had "a big I Love Lucy Vitameatavegimen" poster. Gina explained that, in the episode, Lucy became intoxicated on Vitameatavegimen elixir during the filming of a commercial because she was ordered by the director to do multiple practice-takes, over and over and over again until she could swallow it without making a disgusting looking face. Ultimately, Lucy couldn't accomplish the task—and instead became intoxicated by the elixir. Gina explained that the reason this poster is so funny to her caseworkers is because sometimes they feel like they are expected to repeat instructions and goals over and over with their client, even though they won't be able to follow through on the requests. For example, Gina mentioned that caseworkers like her are expected to continue to offer the same services to repeat offenders and that this is true even when the caseworker already knows the offender has not responded to the service in the "previous take." The Vitameatavegimen meme reminds her to laugh at this aspect of the job instead of getting frustrated.

Phoebe (intake caseworker 9 years and treatment caseworker for 1 year) and her coworkers had a meme related to a specific case referral their office received. The referral involved the discovery and subsequent exposure to a methamphetamine lab in a house. Getting a new referral for a methamphetamine lab is stressful and the task does not come with formal recognition of the dangerous and hard work that must be completed. To acknowledge this stressful type of referral, caseworkers in her office would print a "certificate" which included a meme-pun about meth labs. The caseworkers in her office called the "Lab-MethBusters" certificate which was a pun of the popular television show MythBusters and included a photo of the hosts. Coworkers would post the meme outside the person's cubicle that received a meth lab referral. This was a funny way of acknowledging the dangers encountered with a potential meth lab. Caseworkers creating this informal award, inked with humor, served as informal acknowledgement, and strengthened relationships among coworkers.

Dana (treatment caseworker for 7½ years) and her coworkers also engaged in meme humor to address emotions and stress at another intake office. For Dana's coworkers, just like most caseworkers, there are multiple cases in child welfare that requires them to have a man tested to establish paternity of a child they are working with. This too can be a stressful situation for caseworkers. To acknowledge this, Dana's office had a "Darth Vader" meme on the wall with his well-known revelation "Luke, I am your father!" Dana recalls her coworkers found this post being "pretty funny" when referring to the paternity situations they face at work.

In the same office, Kelly talked about a picture of a pig, that Dana printed and put in her cubicle. Kelly recalled how she was referred to a deplorable home for concerns about sanitary conditions. During the visit, she encountered a 200-pound pig that was allowed to defecate and urinate throughout the house. As a routine process of work, Kelly took photos of the condition of the home and put them into the organization's computer system. As a joke, Dana decided to print out the pictures of the pig and post them in Kelly's cubicle. Dana found such joy and laugher in posting this in her coworker's office and stated that she "will never forget the pig." She went on to state that it "wasn't a good or fun situation" because caseworkers had to help the family find another place to stay while they got a professional to clean the home. She recalls that this is "something that you would think you don't see" unless it is on "TV." However, joking was a way for her to help her coworkers manage the stress associated with the case. The sense of humor that Dana and Kelly used with each other was a positive way to overcome the traumas and dilemmas that they faced, build cohesion, and manage emotions and stressors.

Other office memes had no real meaning behind them. For instance, Crystal (intake caseworker 2 years and 9 months and treatment caseworker for 2 months) said that her coworkers put up a meme photo on the wall that said "1,000,500 days of raptor free attacks." She stated that the post "made no sense" but "it was hilarious" because on the worst days it was at least one thing positive.

The Office of Children, Youth and Families that Christy has been employed at for 20 years engaged in meme humor as well. They posted on their cubical walls a "naughty or nice list" during Christmastime. The list had several of the most unpleasant experiences from the year's case referrals listed on it. She enjoyed scrolling through and looking for her name, finding out who was naughty or nice, and then reading about the case referral details. She looked forward to coming into work "each day" and going to find out "who was added" to the list. Some memorable naughty behaviors she mentioned on the list included "getting greeted by like a pig," "masturbating in a park," and "found guilty flashing someone." Christy said that the list did not include any client's names but did include client behaviors with a coworker's name next to it. Christy recalled that she was kind of upset because she wanted to be on the naughty list because she thought it was "hilarious." She said the posts were not meant to "be mean" or "hurt somebody else's feelings" but just meant to help people vent about the challenges they faced throughout the year. Christy recalled that despite everyone in her unit thinking it was super funny, upper management deemed the list inappropriate and removed it after six days. In hindsight, Christy acknowledged that this was "pretty demented" but that it was their "attempt at humor." In a way, her coworkers were attempting to reframe their dilemmas through humor. It was also a way to bring the caseworkers closer together and allowed them to bond.

Office pranks and meme humor provides caseworkers a mechanism for social solidarity in the office. Pranks and memes, for the most part, created group cohesion and collaboration. Yet, humor also covers up underlying traumas caseworkers are experiencing and, at times, could even undermine solidarity among caseworkers. Organizational leaders and managers should observe how and where this humor appears and use it as a barometer of the agency's culture and how stress and emotions are being managed by their caseworkers. Attention to the humor of the office can help leaders make decisions about their organization. We expand on this later in this chapter. However, let's continue our discussion on how humor manifests itself in the Office of Children, Youth and Families culture.

Deadpan Humor and Professionalism

Can humor aid in making child welfare caseworkers seem more professional to the clients and other professionals they may interact with? Deadpan humor, which is telling a joke with no expression, no emotions, and no change in the tone of their voice may be one type of humor that can (Deadpan, n.d.). In Deadpan humor, it is the emotionally neutral delivery of humor that makes the joke a hit. As caseworkers are working with clients in the field, they are exposed to clients' negative behaviors, deplorable living conditions, as well as ethical dilemmas, which can produce a variety of feelings in caseworkers from surprise to fear, sadness, and disgust. As mentioned previously, it is important for caseworkers to manage their physical emotions and body language so that they can deliver and receive information in a straight forth manner. A core value of social work is to respect others and appear bias free. Therefore, caseworkers need to regulate those feelings so they can be neutral and professional while assisting their clients. Deadpanning humor in the office is complementary to casework precisely because it allows caseworkers to maintain their professional expected demeanor through physical work. It also is a form of practice for being neutral with their clients in the field.

Kelly, who has experience as an intake caseworker for 5 years and a treatment caseworker for 3 years, talked a lot about deadpanning at the "ridiculousness of things" that "are not the norm." She stated that this technique helped her find a way to acknowledge, yet also distance herself from "how some people live and their viewpoints on life." She recalls one mother that had several children and most of them were removed from her custody at certain points due to safety concerns. Kelly found the client to be very forward and open about her sexuality when "most of us . . . in our culture are very closed and . . . don't talk about" their sex lives. In contrast, Kelly's client would always have "sex toys out" during the caseworker visits, had a "stripper pole in the house," and would "flaunt around" in skimpy clothing. Kelly recalls being shocked from always seeing "boobs and butt crack" at her visits. During one visit, Kelly said that the client told her that she left the hospital immediately after giving birth to seek out sex. Kelly said the client recalled that "she told the nurse since she didn't tear [in childbirth] she was going to go get laid now." In discussing the case at the office, she found herself relaying these comments in deadpan humor which led to shocking laughter during "regular conversations at the office." She also would make deadpan comparisons of this extreme case to others. For example, if a caseworker relayed in a report that a client had a baby she would deadpan "well, at least they're not going to go tell the nurse, I just had a baby and didn't tear so I'm going to go get laid now." She stated that this humor actually helped her to maintain her professional demeanor with her client, while simultaneously managing her emotions and stress from the casework back at the office.

Ann (treatment caseworker, 5 years) would also use deadpan humor to maintain her professionalism when her clients would say or do something extreme. She acknowledged that this type of humor was her way of "dealing with things," especially when she was feeling "frustration" and needed to "just kind of let go." She recalls one case where she was working with a family and needed to take custody of the child. Ann mentioned that "anytime" she has "taken a kid from a parent" it is "pretty stressful." Deadpanning humor made the disturbing situation easier "to deal with" and was a form of "relief" and "debriefing" that helped her manage her stress.

Charlotte (intake caseworker, 5 years) also used deadpan humor in preparation for referrals. For instance, she received a referral with concerns for a child that was exposed to the sexual act of fellatio. Charlotte and her coworker's response to the receipt of the referral was a deadpan "ohh great, let's go get this fellatio done" rather than settling into the shock of what the child might have encountered. Charlotte said that deadpanning the referral helped her to prepare for the situation she was about to experience and address emotions of anger that would follow. It also allowed her to talk with the family about the referral in a neutral manner. Charlotte does express feeling "bad" about her deadpan jokes—especially since they are used to cover the anger she feels about children's sexual abuse—but also states that they were the best tool she had to complete particularly difficult referrals.

Caseworkers are exposed to situations and conditions in their referrals that go against social norms. These experiences can be traumatic, and yet caseworkers need to maintain their professional demeanor when completing them. Deadpan humor used in the office and in the field is consistent with a professional identity that requires them to be neutral and helpful to their clients. We must acknowledge that deadpanning is a type of physical work, which also prepares caseworkers emotionally to work in the field and remain professional. Yet, we can see that this type of humor has problems as well. If leaders take notice of this, then this can inform them about how their employees are managing emotions and stress. They can then utilize this information to improve their organization's operation.

Internal Monologue Joking and Caseworker Coping

As you can guess, some humor that caseworkers use in the course of their employment is taboo. Sometimes caseworkers even felt their humor might be considered taboo to others in the office. In some cases, caseworkers were reluctant to share their humor even with their immediate group of coworkers and instead kept it to themselves as internal dialog. This type of humor breached professional expectations by its particularly dark or demeaning character, it also often made light of serious situations and vulnerable people and was not considered sharable even to trustworthy coworkers. As a result, child welfare caseworkers did cognitive work to prevent this type of taboo humor from spilling out unexpectedly. By cognitive work, we mean that the casework had to engage in an internal dialogue after developing something humorous in their head to prevent them from saying what they were thinking aloud. When asked why they chose not to share the humor in their head, most of them expressed concerns about being judged by others or appearing unprofessional. Likewise, they had concerns that this type of humor might get them in trouble or even fired.

Gina (intake caseworker, in social services for 25 years) was exposed to a case situation where she was required to work with a sex offender that had sexually molested several children. When Gina had to talk with the sex offender for an interview, she was experiencing a slew of negative emotions of her own. As she recalled looking across the table at the offender, she said she kept repeating in her head "sick bastard." Despite having difficulty coping with the thought of his behaviors she put aside her own emotions to interview him and make recommendations for counseling. During her encounters she coped with internalized humor she had to cognitively manage. Gina expressed that she would "imagine" herself "dismembering him in some way" and "denutting" him. These images in her head made her laugh to herself and "feel better." She knew that these thoughts may not be perceived as humorous by others—even her coworkers, so she kept them to herself. She was especially concerned about the joke being perceived as a threat and didn't "want to get in trouble for threatening someone."

Steven (intake caseworker, 11 months) also kept humor to himself when he was working with a family with severe mental health issues. He would make comments in his head like "what tree" did "these people fall from." He expressed that it was "ridiculous" that this was the type of "world" he had to "deal with." He recalled one time walking in the home and "they wrote all over their walls with crayons." This reminded him of his previous career as a correction officer and the way inmates used to smear fecal matter on the walls. He thought to himself that it could always be worse, the crayons could be poop. Steven's frustration with the parents was that they "actually reproduced" and "that's even scarier." Steven kept this humor to himself because he thought his coworkers would deem it unprofessional, he did not "want to offend anybody," especially considering that it was about vulnerable adults with mental health issues. Yet, he immediately stated that using humor in his head "keeps me sane."

Phoebe also kept humor inside her head when working with a child that was engaging in bestiality with farm animals. She describes the case as "disturbing." In recalling the humor of the case, she said she placed the child into custody at night and didn't get a good look at the area. She went to meet with him the following day and realized that his "school bus ride" required him to pass "all these farms." She recalls snickering as she thought "it must be tough for him riding to school every day" because he sees so many animals. Phoebe explained that she kept quiet about the humor in her head and didn't share her joke because she wasn't sure if she was using the humor to prevent herself from becoming "emotionally attached to that case" or "just being an asshole."

She mentioned that she became concerned that if she shared her humor, she would appear unprofessional to her coworkers.

Dana (treatment caseworker for 7½ years) shared some of her frustration with having a child who was between six and seven years of age on her case-load. The child was putting "hand sanitizer in his cat's eyes." To herself she joked, "I think your kid's the next Jeffrey Dahmer." She chose not to share this thought with her coworkers because she felt that "it is a real mean thing to say about a kid." However, she didn't feel the humor was an intrusive thought because "there's a lot of truth in humor" and found it actually ben-efited her because "it kind of lessens the blow because you're seeing a kid go down a path. . . . Especially if their parents aren't going to do anything about it. I can't do anything about it. Um, it's kind of one of those things where it's like, gee, I hope I never have to say I told you so." Since Dana could not help with the child or parent's behaviors, she used the humor in her head to manage this issue.

Mandy (intake caseworker for 5½ years and a treatment caseworker for 6 months) also used humorous internal dialogue, that she did not share with others, to address dilemmas at work. She would jokingly say to herself after stressful visits to her cases, "let me just drive my car off the fucking cliff." She found this humorous suicide talk helped her "recognize that this is actu-ally like internally something hard for me personally." Even though this brought her awareness about her own stress she still did not express these jokes aloud "because they're socially inappropriate and someone might actu-ally take action." She implied, in a joking tone, that she did not want to be admitted into a mental health hospital.

EMOTIONS, STRESS, AND HUMOR

The forms of humor experienced by Office of Children, Youth, and Families employees serve several professional purposes. Employee's use of pranks, memes, deadpan humor, and internal dialogue that enables workers to form a sense of solidarity with their colleagues, helps them to maintain a profes-sional demeanor, and provides workers a way to cope with cases that are dif-ficult or upsetting. In this section, we review in greater detail what the humor reveals about how caseworkers manage stress and negative emotions related to their employment.

Child welfare caseworkers need to address negative emotions and stress they are experiencing and do so, in part, through utilizing humor personally and interpersonally. How a caseworker uses humor sheds light on how they are coping, signals whether they are overwhelmed by their experiences, and can help determine if they need therapeutic support. How so? By examining the subject matter of the humor. For instance, caseworkers in this study frequently used humor about high caseloads and paperwork, negative aspects of office environments, difficult case situations that are beyond their control, harmful and counterproductive client behaviors, and case working conditions. The subject matter of their joking also constitutes the major sources of stress for caseworkers and are the largest generators of negative emotions for them as well. Therefore, in this section we review more about the details of how humor occurs within these topics.

High Caseloads and Paperwork

Caseworkers often recall making humorous comments regarding the stress of a high caseload. Gina (intake caseworker, in social services for 25 years) stated that humor "is a really, really good way to let out stress because everybody's running around, freaking out." She went on to mention that there is a "never ever ending gobs of paperwork and you're always scrambling to prioritize what needs done first" and the "only way that you can release that" is through "humor." Some jokes caseworkers shared included the subject matter of frustrations around the need to immediately respond to referrals, intensive paperwork, navigating feuding families, and the intrusive calls and visits that comprise this type of casework. With every case there is also the specter of false allegations or invalid cases that meant that the intensive work would be for naught.

Backstage Humor in Case Situations

Child welfare caseworkers utilize behind the scenes backstage humor to address the stress caused by their encounters with clients related to case situations. If you recall in chapter 1, Crystal and her coworker laughed after seeing her client climb out of the apartment window in her underwear and run to the neighbor's home. We surmised that humor was a backstage coping strategy, hidden from clients and intended solely for insiders, and that Crystal and her coworker used it to reduce the stress and frustrations of dealing with a noncompliant client. Other caseworkers in the study also used humor about case situations to address their stressors and emotions.

After receiving a referral about children residing in an unsanitary home, Evelyn (intake caseworker for 4 to 5 years and a treatment caseworker for 2 months) and her coworker, Macy, used backstage humor to cope with feelings of shock and disgust they felt from assessing the family. In their referral investigation, they encountered dog feces throughout the home, in the children's room, and even on top of the beds. Once the two caseworkers left the home, and were alone driving, they joked about the housing conditions.

They both made jokes comparing its smell as worse than the smell from the goat farm next door. Macy then asked Evelyn to stop somewhere to use the restroom on the way to the next referral. Evelyn replied to Macy, "why didn't you just piss on their floor in there, they do? Like it would not have mattered." The two laughed hysterically at the idea of doing so. Evelyn said that this type of joking helped her to shake off the shock from experiencing the conditions of squalor and quickly prepared her for the shocks that may be coming in the next case.

Case situations can also create intense emotional dilemmas for caseworkers that must be managed to remain professional. To do this, they sometimes use backstage humor. Violet (intake caseworker for 5 years and treatment caseworker for 1 year) noted that backstage she may "say things that are really inappropriate in regard to the stuff we see." For instance, her office received a case referral to investigate an apparent suicide from a gunshot wound of a parent while the children were still in the home. Violet was assigned to the team charged with the responsibility of removing the children from the home, ensuring their safety, and that their needs were met. The removal was ordered immediately and took place while the police investigation into the suicide was taking place. When Violet and her team of coworkers arrived, the death scene was not completely cleaned, and she had to step and pivot around the blood and brain matter splattered about the house to get to the children. Helping with the children and comforting them was no easy task, and Violet recalls her coworkers becoming overwhelmed with horror and sickened from the scene. Violet attempted to snap her coworkers from their emotions by making normalizing remarks during the removal such as "it's not the worst house we ever been [in]" or "it's just a little bit of, you know, fluids and stuff." Later, Violet's coworkers recounted these remarks to her backstage, along with detailed descriptions of the actual horrific situation the caseworkers and children were exposed to. Violet acknowledged that these backstage comments, and the ensuing laughter they caused among the caseworkers, were a method to managing residual emotions from the case situation they were faced with.

Client's Behaviors

Client behavior is another common source of stress for caseworkers and for backstage joking. For all caseworkers in child welfare, one of the main charges of the occupation is to assist families, which includes coaching to modify behaviors of clients that are deemed undesirable by the courts. For multiple reasons, helping address behavioral change in child welfare case situations can be stressful. To mitigate this stress, caseworkers stated they use backstage humor with each other about aspects of behavioral change work—often related to the lack of progress in their clients. Using humor provides them with relief from stress and negative emotions and provides them with the ability to dismiss some of the stress from failure.

One detailed example of this comes from Jewel (intake, treatment, and general caseworker for over 12 years) who recalls using various types of humor about her clients to mitigate stress. If you recall her story in a previous chapter, she was working with the pregnant mother struggling with drug abuse and having trouble properly caring for her children. This case was particularly salient because Jewel created a repertoire of jokes about her client to mitigate her frustrations. First, Jewel expressed the frustration that her client's children were perpetually being referred to the child welfare system in the first place. She viewed the persistence of the client's drug abuse problems as the major source of her inability to properly parent her children. Finding herself unable to control the birth mother's drug abuse, Jewel joked with other caseworkers about the case as a way of managing the negative emotions she felt from her client's inability to exact behavioral change. Jewel and her coworkers created running jokes about her client having more children to replace her other children that were removed from the home and under the care of child welfare. Remember that Jewel would joke with others in the office, "how stupid can one be if you don't have your own child now why would you bring another child into this world and think that you're going to keep this child." Lack of control in this part of the job can be incredibly frustrating, however, Jewel—and others—often created backstage joking about the behaviors of the client to deflect blame for their clients' lack of progress.

Jewel also made backstage jokes about this client's appearance as well. If you recall, Jewel made jokes about the client. She said her client "looked like a drug user with terrible teeth," weighed seventy-five pounds, smelled bad, and was disheveled. Jewel joked about this by wondering aloud how any man would desire sex with her. Jewel said she would joke in the same way about this with her coworkers by saying with fake jealously that "she gets more men than me." Jewel admitted that this backstage joking about her client's appearance "made me feel better somehow." This joking was a way for her to address her client's behavior, which she had no control over.

Jewel also admitted that she joked backstage about the woman's drug addiction, which was beyond her control. She recalls joking with her coworkers about the client's poor excuses for failing drug tests. She would retell coworkers how the client feigning ignorance that "she never used them [drugs]" or how she was surprised that "she didn't know how it got into her system." Jewel admitted that the jokes she made about this particularly difficult client to her coworkers "didn't necessarily lift my spirits" but that it provided her with a "mental escape." For Jewel joking about her client helped her reframe the perpetual failures of her client to follow the court orders and to change. The backstage joking became an outlet of stress relief. For Jewel, joking about this client with her coworkers was "basically one thing that got me through it." As you might figure, this type of backstage joking due to lack of control of your client's behaviors, although personally helpful, raises concerns and poses challenges to professional ethics.

Toni (treatment caseworker, 10 years) also found herself using dark humor backstage in a case where a child was a victim of gang rape. During her handling of the case, the teenager (15 years) ran away from home to have sex with another adult, Toni explained. This complicated the investigation and frustrated Toni because she now had an additional criminal case to address in her investigation report. In addition, the details of the case made the local news when the child went missing, which added another layer of pressure for Toni. This was further compounded during the course of the investigation when the child continued to run away over and over, and each time she would have sex with another adult in a different jurisdiction. Part of the additional work this created for Toni is that every time a crime is committed in a new jurisdiction, it necessitates a new investigation. Therefore, since the child kept having sex with adults in different homes and locations, this required Toni to collaborate with police and other authorities across multiple jurisdictions. As the complexity of the case grew, Toni found herself by the end of it all having loads of extra sets of paperwork to complete and a multipronged chain of professionals and agencies to coordinate with. Additionally, this put her into the high-pressure situations of navigating and learning new reporting systems just to keep up with the requirements of the case. As a result of the stress, Toni began making jokes backstage to coworkers about the child's incorrigibility in running away. Toni said that she would purposely avoid acknowledging the aspect of child rape in her backstage joking about the child even though it was clear to her that the crime and subsequent behaviors were tied together. She said that the jokes about running away "again and again" helped her to manage the stress and negative emotions she was experiencing about how this behavior was complicating her work.

IMPACTS OF HUMOR

So far, we've learned that caseworkers use humor in the form of pranks, games, nonverbal humor, deadpan humor, and in an internal dialog that they do not share with others. Humor provides a mechanism for social solidarity, is a tool that helps maintain professional demeanor, and aids them at managing their own feelings and experience of stress. The subject of the humor is mostly centered around high caseloads, paperwork, case situations beyond their control, troublesome client behaviors and emotions, and difficult working conditions. We have also alluded to the fact that humor produces negative and positive outcomes for the individual, groups of caseworkers, and the organization. In the following section, we review exactly what caseworkers say about the impacts of humor.

Humor Provides Relief

In our study participants generally stated that humor provides relief from the stress and negative emotions that build as a result of being a child welfare caseworker. Nora (an intake caseworker for 7 months and a treatment caseworker for over 4 years) said directly that when it comes to humor, "it relieves us as workers because we're always like, so stressed and going in the most chaotic environments that we need the relief to, like, step back and just like, say how like weird and crazy these situations are." Ella went on to say it is as if humor is a "shield" and a way to get the stress out without "reliving the trauma" (Ella, intake caseworker for 2½ years). Trish (intake caseworker for between 2 and 3 years and a treatment caseworker for 1 year) thinks that humor is a "relief that a lot of people use at the agency . . . to get through pretty tough case[s] or removal[s] of a child because that's never easy." She went on to explain "once you see the dark side [of cases] . . . if you can't laugh about it, and you take it home, it gets to weighing on you."

Trish revealed a specific type of case situation that she is exposed to frequently, which she uses humor to relieve her from emotions and stress due to the situation. She said that caseworkers at her agency constantly work with children that have headlice. Yes, the dreaded headlice. If you have ever been exposed to this, you know the irritation. There are concerns among caseworkers about preventing bringing lice infestation home to their own families. There are also concerns about the extra sanitation work needed in the prevention efforts. Trish noted that caseworkers are not given extra time for this type of cleaning. As a result, the running office joke when a caseworker is assigned to meet a family with headlice is about the inevitability of bringing the infestation home. This accompanies "warnings" about getting their car infested with lice. They jokingly remind each other "you better tuck your pants in your socks and spray before you get in there." This humor provides Trish with a "release."

Kelly, who has experience as an intake caseworker for 5 years and a treatment caseworker for 3 years, also acknowledges that humor is a way to "de-stress" as well as "talk about things without getting super emotional." Kelly describes her job as having "high stress" and her office as a "safety zone" where she is not "afraid to laugh or joke around." Kelly said her ability to use humor is important to be able to do her job. She even recruited another coworker from the first agency she worked at to transfer to her current employer because "it makes a big difference when you can use humor and not be stressed out while you're in the office as well as out of the office." Kelly went on to say that if it were not for the use of humor, she would not be able to get her "stress level down" and could have a "mental breakdown" because of the "awful" and "ridiculous things" that she is exposed to in her casework.

Humor as Emotion Work

Not only do child welfare caseworkers say humor is a stress relief, but they also say they use it to brush off negative emotions. Trish explained that child welfare caseworkers can "internalize . . . the stuff that goes on" and this could "drive people crazy." So, workers must "laugh about it and roll it off [their] chest." She uses humor as an emotional "defense mechanism" to "laugh it off" in a way that it "is a forefront feeling that may be covering up something else." Lily (intake caseworker for 2½ years and a treatment caseworker for 3 years) also used humor "to get through" her work because if she did not laugh, she would "end up crying forever." Betty (treatment caseworker, 3 years) explained that she uses humor when she witnesses "pictures of physically abused kids," deals with conflicts with the legal team, or has a bad day at court. Humor "doesn't change the situation" but it allows her to take some of the emotion out of the situation so she can move on. Humor is her way to "talk about it without having to really talk about it." Harper (intake caseworker 1 year and treatment caseworker 1 year) recalls that she was emotional in the beginning of her career but after three or four months, she started to use humor. She said it took the "emotional part out" of the job, prevented getting "emotionally attached" to her cases, and helped her "move on" with her work. The humor, for her, took the "pressure off" and helped her "distance [herself] from the emotions of the case and just like keep it professional."

Jade (a general caseworker for 6 years) expanded on the ability of humor to brush off negative emotions. She explained that "if you don't laugh" you can "internalize a lot," then "it becomes harder to do your job and then you get higher turnover." She thinks it is important to ensure that her emotions do not get to her, therefore she lets "humor takeover" to "protect" herself. In greater detail, Jade said:

> Laughing about something as stupid as [the disbelief in what] a client wore to court. . . . I have this running joke with my supervisor that some days I wish Joan Rivers would just come back to life and do [her bit on] Fashion Police at the courthouse. Because I would just love to hear her commentary of some of the outfits you see there. . . . But if you don't laugh and you internalize it . . . you feel it more. You create like this numbing barrier with humor . . . where you stop your emotions at a point where you don't get too emotionally involved.

Humor Covers Up Trauma

Although stress relief and emotion work can be viewed as a positive aspect of humor for participants, the examples illustrate that there may be some cover up of the trauma child welfare caseworkers experience. Earlier, Trish noted that she thinks "laughter and humor . . . may be covering up something else." When she was asked what she thought it was covering up, she said "sadness" and "it's stressful thinking about how you are responsible for families . . . for children. It is stressful worrying about if you did everything that you could have." She explained that "covering all that up" with "laughter" allows her to go home without crying each day.

Evelyn's use of humor also covered up some of the trauma she experienced to the extent that she did not even realize all the trauma she had experienced until she left her job. She explained that the job is so busy, and it is hard to find time to fully process all your experiences, traumas, dilemmas, emotions, and stressors. When she left her job, it took her "six months of sitting in my backyard by myself, usually with a case of beer." She stated that "I didn't like anybody, let alone want to be around anybody. I had lost my faith in humanity. Lost my faith in humor. Lost my faith in myself. Because [once I left] it wasn't funny anymore." She went on to state "when you can't laugh, you just go crazy." She feels like she is a "very strong" person that can "handle a lot of things." However, she did not even realize all the "vicarious trauma" she was exposed to until she left the job. She stated that she finally saw it when she would "sit down and actually just rest." She describes the whole experience as being weird, in that it takes a long time to understand this and there comes a point when you don't "even really like yourself" anymore.

Humor Alters Personal Identity

Olivia (treatment caseworker for 5 years) also expressed that humor masked some of the trauma she has experienced. Humor helped her "shut" her "emotions off." She explained that humor can be used to "cope so you do not burnout or take it home with you." It is for these reasons that she "learned to use [the joking] to shut emotions off" so she could "actually enjoy home life and life outside work." She recalls attending her grandmother's funeral and just sitting there emotionless while her sister was "a mess." Her sister told Olivia that she needed "to turn her emotions back on." However, it was "not that easy." Olivia was alluding to the fact that—in Goffman's terms, the mask she wore had become her face—and the humor not only covered up trauma, it altered her sense of self.

Abigail (intake, 3 years) recalls having a hard time transitioning from educational and professional standards to the reality of the field noting that

over time her "outlook on people, in general, has changed." When she was
in school for social work, professors taught "people first, strength based, and
trauma focused" and reiterated "that all people are good." She then dismissed
this perspective by stating her professors were "out of touch." She went on to
say that the use of humor to address stress is "real life" and it is not "realistic
to find the good in everybody all the time." She acknowledged however that
even though "using dark humor" or "talking negatively about clients" helps
relieve stress, it "kind of takes us away from the mission but at the same
time none of us would have made it in our job as long as we have without
it." Abigail noted how working in child welfare changed parts of her identity,
which gave her conflicting messages about what her professional training was
preparing her for.

Jade (a general caseworker for 6 years) had similar experiences of her identity being altered, but also felt the need to continue to use humor. As a result,
she did not feel at liberty to share humor with everyone. Before she started
working as a child welfare caseworker, she described her humor as being
"Disney humor" which she explained as "light and sweet and flowery and
princesses and bubbly." Once she started to work as a caseworker her "Disney
princesses" humor transformed to "Mel Brooks" humor. Her new reality was
laughing at "really dark morbid things," and she quickly realized that she
could not share it with people in her personal life. This left her in a "lonely,
dark place where everyone's telling jokes, you're like, I have so many funny
jokes, but you wouldn't get them because you don't think a grandmother with
dementia wearing a ball gown is hilarious. You think it's sad." Violet (intake
caseworker for 5 years and treatment caseworker for 1 year) also expressed
a change in her identity because of her work in child welfare. She describes
her job as making her "look at things a lot differently than a normal person
in society would." Her "different view on things" caused her to "normalize
things that she shouldn't." She remarked that "people hurting kids isn't funny,
but we have to deal with that individually . . . and we joke about that, not
about what they did, but the person in general or the situation."

Sometimes caseworker's friends and family, outside of child welfare,
have picked up on the identity change surrounded in the dark humor of child
welfare. Sabrina (intake caseworker, 2 years) recalls conversations with her
mother and fiancé about how she has changed due to her work as a caseworker. Her mother tells her that her job has "dulled" her "sparkles" and both
her mother and fiancé have said the job has "ruined" her. This caused her to
separate certain aspects of her life from others. Harper (intake caseworker
for 1 year and treatment caseworker for 1 year) also hears about how she has
changed from her family. Her family has told her to "chill out" because she is
"being darker than usual." Olivia's mom also started to notice a change in her
daughter. She told Olivia that she has "no emotions, because" she "laugh[s]

about everything" that is "inappropriate." The job, as well as the humor, has changed caseworker's identity and those close to them have taken notice. In some incidents, the relationships and connections that caseworkers have with people outside of the child welfare system have been impacted because the humor is not valued outside of their work.

Rose "learned early on" not to use the same subject of humor outside of her work circle, because "people would not understand." In discussing her use of humor, Hazel (a treatment caseworker for 2 years) revealed that the "job becomes who you are, not just what you do." She said that her personality changed over time, and she would find herself "kind of shutting down when I'm like, out with like, normal people." This was in part not wanting to say anything that was "inappropriate or stupid" and then "beating yourself up for saying something that like, probably wasn't appropriate." She found that the "people in the office are the people who really understand what she is going through" and felt the freedom to joke with them about anything.

Crystal (intake caseworker for 2 years and 9 months and treatment caseworker for 2 months) acknowledges that the sense of humor she developed on the job was a factor that contributed to her divorce. She stated that she used to think her ex-husband was the "asshole" of the couple but over the "the last ten years" she realized that she was "an asshole because of [her] job." She explained that she could not talk freely with her ex-husband about her experiences in social work because he was not in "social services."

Other caseworkers said they had similar, less extreme, experiences of distance from loved ones because of the sense of humor they developed from work. For instance, some learned to not talk about their employment with loved ones, and other caseworkers chose to filter themselves when discussing work. For instance, Jewel (intake, treatment, and general caseworker for over 12 years) used humor about her job with her husband, but she would filter out the "sad things" because she perceived it was traumatizing for him to hear. So, she only showed parts of her sense of humor to him and "keep it light." She compared her situation to her mother's job at a bank. Her mother complains about her negative work experiences. Jewel said that all she can think about when this happens is that her mother doesn't realize that her work involves investigations of children dying from abuse and neglect. Even with a filter, she found it hard to connect with others and to sympathize with their situations and stressors.

SUMMARY

Throughout this chapter, we have explored how intake and treatment caseworkers use humor and gallows humor, and what that reveals about how they are managing stress and emotions related to their employment. As well as the first part of our second research question: What are the negative and positive effects of the use of gallows humor among individuals? We found that humor occurs among child welfare caseworkers through pranks, games, nonverbal humor, deadpan humor, and humor that is used within a caseworker's own mind. These methods of humor provide social solidarity, the ability to maintain professional demeanor, and a way to manage one's own feelings cognitively. Caseworkers use these methods of humor to provide them relief from negative emotions, which was usually due to high caseload and paperwork, environmental issues, case situations that are beyond their control, client behaviors and emotions, and working conditions. This only confirms that caseworkers are dealing with dilemmas that are a source of stress and negative emotions for them. However, humor to cope with stress and manage emotions has both positive and negative impacts on the individual. Humor can be beneficial due to its ability to provide caseworkers with relief from stress and negative emotions in relation to their employment. Humor also provides them with a way to brush off negative emotions and stress created by the dilemmas they experience. Nonetheless, humor does have the negative impacts of covering up traumas, altering child welfare caseworkers' identity and affecting connections with those that are not employed in the profession.

Chapter 5

Humor amid Groups

In the last chapter, we mainly focused on what humor does for child welfare workers at the individual level, which is only part of the full story. We covered this to establish an initial understanding and provide examples of the impacts of humor among groups of child welfare caseworkers. The stage is now set to explore more about what humor does for these organizations more generally. In this chapter, we do this and provide an answer to the second part of our second research question: What are the negative and positive effects of the use of humor among child welfare worker groups and the organization? We will then examine our third research question in chapter 6, Are there any similarities and/or differences between how intake and treatment employees utilize humor?

We assert that humor benefits the organization by building group cohesion, facilitating collaboration, and preventing burnout. However, humor can also be a detriment in facilitating unprofessional and ethically fraught behavior during referral investigations and in the course of case management. We discuss these findings about group and organizational level impacts of humor, calling back to some examples from the previous chapters as well as bringing some new ones out from our interview study.

A focus on humor at the group and organizational levels provides an overall picture and understanding of humor in the group dynamic at Office of Children, Youth and Families. We find that organizational leaders manage their employees' use of humor in both permissive and restrictive forms which vary among the two different office roles. We focus specifically on how this impacts the trend of intake caseworkers tending to use darker humor more frequently and treatment caseworkers tending to use humor directly with their clients.

HUMOR BUILDS COHESION AND COLLABORATION

"A sense of humor is part of the art of leadership, of getting along with people, of getting things done." Dwight D. Eisenhower's memorable quote above about how humor can be a tool that leaders use to build collaboration and develop group cohesion rings true with child welfare workers. In fact, our study supports previous research findings that humor reciprocally supports group cohesion among child protective caseworkers (Howell, 2008). Caseworkers in this study used humor to build trust and cohesion with each other, which differs from the expectation that it was used among caseworkers that already had built trust. The findings showed how humor, rather than being a product of trust and cohesion, is a tool for developing cohesion and trust.

Our participants regularly highlighted the value of humor to build trust and cohesion with coworkers. For instance, Novah (a treatment caseworker for 1½ years) explained her humor provides the ability to open the "line of communication" with others and form relationships and friendships. Toni (treatment caseworker, 10 years) expressed "when we laugh about things, I mean . . . it's nice being able to laugh about things and feeling like you're not the only one that can find the humor in it. So you do feel bonded in a way." For her "just being able to be there" for coworkers "through a situation" with the use of laugher "makes them feel better." Others felt that humor produces a deeper "relationship with each other," builds "morale," creates an "incredible bond" and reassures caseworkers that no matter what, they have each "other's back" (Mandy, intake caseworker for 5½ years and a treatment caseworker for 6 months). These findings support literature about humor's ability to promote bonding (Mesmer-Magnus, Glew & Chockalingam, 2012).

Humor is a vehicle of support to colleagues. Isabella (intake caseworker for 1½ years) stated that she and her coworkers use humor to share case experiences. Presenting case experiences in a humorous light helped her breach seemingly sensitive topics with others and learn if they interpreted the situation the same way. For her, using humor helped to avoid fear of judgment when talking about how she might handle the aspects of a case. She said that this technique helped to eventually feel greatly supported among her coworkers. However, Isabella noted that it didn't work with her supervisor. She said her supervisor didn't understand her use of humor, and that if he did, she would have felt more "supported and heard." Other caseworkers expressed similar sentiments that humor didn't work the same with management, yet they still found it quite valuable to build relationships with other professionals in the community that they work with.

Participants said that the use of humor supported collaboration between other professionals outside of the agency as well. Using humor to build trust and cohesion with other professionals provides child welfare caseworkers with a means for collaboration on case referrals and investigations. Abigail (intake caseworker, 3 years) noted that she has built a relationship with a local hospital social worker by making "off the record joke[s] about stuff" on common cases they have shared. For instance, they will joke around about how a client is "crazy" or comment on the odd aspects of their case. Abigail said that a few times they ended up laughing so hard they started crying. Abigail said that participating in this humor with the hospital social worker solidifies that both have the "same mission" and "feel the same" way towards their work. Abigail reassured that this type of joking ultimately led both of them to understand that they "really feel bad" and "care about" the clients in the same way, which made case burdens and decision making easier.

Novah also said that her use of humor with external human service providers facilitates relationships and aids in collaboration. For her humor "helps bring things into perspective" and ensures that she is on the "same page" as the other providers. For example, she had a case she was working on with an outside human service provider. They would use humor together to work on making decisions which gave them the ability to "understand each other better." Similarly, Gina (intake caseworker, in social services for 25 years) also recalls a case where she used humor with law enforcement that had positive outcomes. She and an officer she was working with would make references to the television show "The World's Dumbest Criminals" when discussing clients which gave both of them a "sense of bonding and understanding" that they were feeling similar about the issues arising in the case. It helped her with building trust with the officer which led to increased information sharing. In general, caseworkers said that humor was a quick and easy tool for facilitating collaboration with others outside their agency.

HUMOR PROMOTES WORKFLOW

Another positive aspect of humor that occurs at the organizational level is its ability to support and encourage timely workflow. Humor provides caseworkers with the opportunity to form relationships that in return provides them with the capability to ask others for help when needed. This has implications for leaders to harness this as a tool when creating appropriate training and wellness programs for their staff.

When caseworkers establish work relationships through humor, they can then use those relationships to complete their work in a timely fashion (Craun & Bourke, 2014; Johnson, 2007; Obrdlik, 1942). Novah mentioned that humor gave her the ability to form bonds which allowed her to more freely "ask others for help when I needed it." She said that even though caseworkers are all assigned their own referrals, their high demands and complicated nature dictate a reliance on each other to assist in managing them. Novah said that on more than one occasion she has capitalized on the relationships she has built through humor to resolve her referrals in compliance with policies, regulations, and laws.

Not only does humor aid workflow by making it easier to ask others for help, but it also relieves the type of stress that prevents clarity of thinking and in communication. Quinton, intake caseworker for 1 year and treatment caseworker for 6 years, said that he feels work is "incredibly stressful" and sometimes stress can cause him to "shut down." Laughing and joking with others provides a method to "decrease stress" and make his "brain work a little bit easier" so "better decisions can be made." Quinton's statement is supported by research showing that humor can reduce stress, provide emotion management, and can help complete job-related tasks (Craun & Bourke, 2014; Johnson, 2007; Obrdlik, 1942). For Dana (treatment caseworker for 7½ years) humor allows her to "take a deep breath" and do her job with others.

Participants also stated that humor has the capacity to reduce office tension that thereby increases workflow. Caseworkers experienced "unpleasant" feelings in the office as a result of their work and pointed to humor as the "outlet" for reducing these feelings (Toni, treatment caseworker for 10 years). For Toni, humor changes the atmosphere, preventing her "from getting overwhelmed and burned out." She gave the example of trying to laugh about situations she encounters because if she "hold[s] it inside" then "it can create a lot of anger and tension" that can impact her work. Violet (intake caseworker for 5 years and treatment caseworker for 1 year) mentioned that humor allows her "to continue to do" her work by "normalizing" her experiences through humor and deal with "secondary trauma," so that she can "continue" with her work and reduce the likelihood of her getting "burnout." These testimonies of our participants supports research on humor as a method to prevent burnout (Scott, 2007).

As we have discussed, humor has positive impacts on groups and the organization by encouraging workflow. Participants said the ease and pace of workflow increased from relationships formed through humor. This tool allowed caseworkers to ask others for help, address stress and emotions, and jointly help them decrease burnout. But what are the negative impacts of humor on the organization? In the next section, we explore how the use of humor necessitates the need to monitor it and how humor leads to behaviors that are unprofessional and challenge ethics.

HUMOR REQUIRES MONITORING

Have you ever told a joke where everyone in the room breaks out into laughter? It feels great, right? You are smiling, connecting with others, and enjoying all that a joke has to offer. But have you ever told a joke where no one laughs? The awkwardness, isolation from others, and embarrassment can be overwhelming. This can be the case if the joke is not funny but imagine if it is also offensive to someone.

The content of joking among caseworkers can be considered quite sensitive and many caseworkers in our study had concerns about offending others and fears of repercussion due to causing offense. We found that caseworkers often experience conflicted feelings from their humor. They also expressed concerns and shared stories about being disciplined by management for humor leading to a "toe in the water" approach to see how others respond to their attempts at humor. We found that employees spend time and energy monitoring theirs and others humor in the office that could be expended elsewhere. In this section, we review examples of concerns with offending others, the judgment it causes, potential conflicts, testing humor, and being disciplined for it all as methods for monitoring humor within the organization.

Gallows humor can be offensive and insensitive (Coughlin, 2002) and judgments can also cause conflict among employees thereby creating a need to continue to monitor their humor. As such, caseworkers monitor their humor as a routine part of their job. Child welfare caseworkers expressed concerns about their humor offending others and being judged by them due to it. Betty (treatment caseworker, 3 years) explained that sometimes "what you think is funny, other people might not think is funny." She recalls a time a coworker made a humorous comment about the circumstances surrounding a "kiddo overdosing and dying." Betty reported that she may have found this "funnier" on another day, but she recently had another coworker confide in her that they lost a cousin because of an overdose. This led to a temporary strain in the working relationship among the group as a result. Christy (who has been employed at the Office of Children, Youth and Families for 20 years) echoed that this experience is common for coworkers to be offended by other coworkers' humor and this makes her "frustrated" because a joke about a traumatic experience signals they need support rather than being judged for appearing to be "unglued."

Naomi, an intake caseworker for 5 years and treatment caseworker for 3 years, mentioned that there are times during meetings with clients, when intake caseworkers and treatment caseworkers will talk beforehand. She recalls times that the intake caseworker would say "something to the treatment worker in that joking, dirty, twisted humor about the family. Um you know about that crazy dad, oh, you better watch out, he's going to get you, or you better watch out. He's gonna, you know, drop his pants." Then the treatment caseworkers would go back to their supervisor and report that the intake caseworker used "twisted" humor and they "can't believe they said that." Humor does have the potential to cause some separation and judgment among those that do not use the same humor. Naomi mentioned that because of humor like this she has a "bad taste in their mouth about that intake worker, because you know, they just don't understand."

Evelyn (intake caseworker for 4 to 5 years and a treatment caseworker for 2 months) stated that intake caseworkers use darker humor, and this sometimes creates conflict, because treatment caseworkers don't understand and are offended due to their ongoing relationship with their clients. She recalls that one of her coworkers had been in the treatment department for years and had never really been exposed to a "dirty house." She was offended by the humor that the intake caseworkers used about dirty homes. However, one day her coworker transferred to the intake department, and wouldn't you know it, she had to assess a dirty home. During her visit at the dirty home, she found a cockroach frozen in the freezer. It was actually frozen in the ice cube tray. Evelyn and her new intake coworker laughed about the situation. They would make body and facial expressions like they were wide-eyed and frozen dead cockroaches. However, Evelyn mentioned that when her coworker was in the treatment department she would have never used or understood this type of humor. Due to intakes "gross sense of humor" (which we discuss in more detail later under the difference between the two departments section) they can be seen as "insensitive" which can cause a "rift" among the two departments. Not only can humor cause conflict between two departments, but it can also cause frustration between genders.

Peter (intake caseworker, 3 years) remarked that he was a "male in a female dominant world." Sometimes for him, humor made him feel uncomfortable. He was not sure how to handle women joking about the topics that his female coworkers were talking about. He was accustomed to women being more reserved. For him, female caseworkers were far more crude with their jokes than what he has heard in male locker rooms. Peter was not sure how to manage and deal with the humor that was being used around him and he felt a disconnect. He was also timid to participate in humor with his female coworkers for fear that he could offend them or even worse get in trouble with management.

If humor is not monitored there is a potential to have conflict with others. Charlotte, an intake caseworker for 5 years, experienced this firsthand. Charlotte recalls a time when she was joking around with a coworker that she did not know well. At the time she was not closely monitoring her humor, however she thought the jokes were going well. I imagine she felt like she was the world's greatest comedian, landing joke after joke, and helping others find joy in this in this big fishbowl we call life. She reported that she felt like she made a connection with an unfamiliar coworker. An hour went by, and Charlotte said something humorous again but this time it was to another coworker. She smiled at her comic skill landing once again. However, the unfamiliar coworker overheard the joke. This time the coworker felt that the humor was "inappropriate" and "was like, I'm done with you." Charlotte recalls the situation being "really blown out of proportion" and if the coworker knew Charlotte and her "personality" they would know her type of humor was "not meant" to hurt anyone and was "just a joke." As a result of this confrontational situation, Charlotte and the unfamiliar coworker remained just that, unfamiliar. Charlotte mentioned that she avoided the coworker unless she had to talk to them.

Not all caseworkers in this study experienced conflict due to the use of humor. Lily (intake caseworker for 2½ years and a treatment caseworker for 3 years) mentioned that she does not think there is a lot of conflict due to humor. She noted that perhaps this is because there are "clicks" of people that would use their type of humor together. "You would see groups of people who kind of had that same humor" that would "congregate together." This would "especially" occur "at lunch or social events." Rose also expressed that she does not recall any conflicts due to humor, but she does recall disagreeing with other caseworkers at times and understands how there could be a "potential" for conflict.

Not only does a lack of monitoring humor have the potential to divide coworkers and create conflict but it can also result in informal disciplinary actions. Isabella (intake caseworker for 1½ years) would experience what she felt was judgment from her supervisor about her humor. She mentioned her supervisor would look at her "shocked" as if they were saying "how dare you" when she laughed at certain things. Isabella would initially say to herself "oh, mom's mad, I'm in trouble" although she got an unsettling feeling inside that her supervisor thought she was actually "a heartless monster." She began to monitor herself more around her supervisor, which she admitted impacted her work output and morale. Jewel, Christy, and Susan also expressed fear of getting in trouble from management due to their use of humor. Jewel recalled a time that a treatment supervisor reprimanded the three of them because a treatment worker was offended by the humor. The supervisor approached the caseworkers and said,

> Hey, I just wanted to let you know that [your colleague] brought this to my attention. That she's really struggling on the floor because she's constantly hearing people talk crap on clients, and it really offends her. She doesn't think that

we're being professional, and I want to give you guys a heads up. You may want to talk to your team and tell them to knock it off.

Jewel recalls thinking, "I'm not talking to my team, because if people get through the day with humor, then so be it." For her, humor is the way case-workers "survive."

As we have established, humor is something that caseworkers see as essential to their job but must monitor around others. Beyond self-monitoring, caseworkers closely observe how others around them are using humor. They often test humor out with people while assessing their response to see whether others interpret the humor differently than intended. For instance, Crystal stated that she "kind of tests the water" by throwing a humorous line out to check for other's response. Trish gave a more detailed example of testing her sense of humor with others at work. Trish stated that she nicknamed a coworker "Black Joe," which she made as a combination of the coworker's name "Joe" with his race "Black." Trish's coworker Joe told her that he finds the joke funny and innocent, but some caseworkers in her office castigated her as racially insensitive. So, to avoid further conflicts, Trish started censoring her humor around some of her coworkers by probing her coworkers with various degrees of offensiveness to see how they would react. She also noted when others told jokes around her. For her, this tells her if she must be serious around them or if she can joke with that person.

Self-monitoring humor can become burdensome for child welfare caseworkers who feel like they are just trying to manage their stress while completing job tasks. Similarly, organizational monitoring of humor can have a negative impact on the agency as manager's attention gets diverted from monitoring other organizational tasks. Yet the need for monitoring is confounded at the organizational level because some use of humor is unprofessional, challenges caseworker ethics, and causes internal conflict for child welfare caseworkers.

INTERNAL CONFLICT

Caseworkers often feared that their humor could be perceived as unprofessional and a breach of ethical principles. Perhaps this is due to it being viewed by outsiders as offensive, insensitive, and inappropriate (Coughlin, 2002). Child welfare caseworker education fields such as social work, human services, sociology, and psychology often neglect discussion of the role of humor in the workplace. When they are discussed, it is often in the form of blanket statements that it is not appropriate and ethical behavior. The National Association of Social Workers, NASW, core values are service, social justice, dignity and worth of the person, importance of human relationships, integrity, and competence (National Association of Social Workers, 2023). The NASW has a code of ethics that social workers are introduced to in college. The NASW (2023) states that the NASW Code of Ethics serves six purposes:

1. The Code identifies core values on which social work's mission is based.
2. The Code summarizes broad ethical principles that reflect the profession's core values and establishes a set of specific ethical standards that should be used to guide social work practice.
3. The Code is designed to help social workers identify relevant considerations when professional obligations conflict or ethical uncertainties arise.
4. The Code provides ethical standards to which the general public can hold the social work profession accountable.
5. The Code socializes practitioners new to the field to social work's mission, values, ethical principles, and ethical standards, and encourages all social workers to engage in self-care, ongoing education, and other activities to ensure their commitment to those same core features of the profession.
6. The Code articulates standards that the social work profession itself can use to assess whether social workers have engaged in unethical conduct. NASW has formal procedures to adjudicate ethics complaints filed against its members. In subscribing to this Code, social workers are required to cooperate in its implementation, participate in NASW adjudication proceedings, and abide by any NASW disciplinary rulings or sanctions based on it.

The Code includes ethical responsibilities to the client, colleagues, practice setting, professionals, social work profession, and the broader society (National Association of Social Workers, 2023). Although humor is not directly addressed, there are some sections that can muddy the water about ethics and humor. For instance, there is a section that addressed derogatory language with clients and another section that talks about unethical conduct with colleagues (National Association of Social Workers, 2023).

Nora (an intake caseworker for 7 months and a treatment caseworker for over 4 years) recalls being taught in college that it is inappropriate to laugh on the job as a social worker. When asked about the specifics of the lesson she mentioned that she was just taught in blanket fashion that professionals could not use humor, especially joking about the client. She stated that it was taught in the context of a discussion of "confidentiality and like ethics in general." She went on to state her professor told her that she "shouldn't be talking about your clients to your coworkers anyways, because they're not their clients."

Hazel (a treatment caseworker for 2 years) noted that new caseworkers straight from college are "professional and very ethical." She observed that new caseworkers often view seasoned caseworker humor as "disrespectful to families" and "unprofessional." Hazel also observed that caseworkers who fail to adopt this approach after a while "will not last long." She stated that new hires learn that humor is a balancing act, "if you use too much or not [at] the right time it can come off pretty unprofessional" but that using no humor on the job at all can be stifling.

Humor as unprofessional behavior is often brought into a tension with caseworker culture and its utility in managing stress and negative emotion. We identify a large professional gray area since caseworker education and ethics proscribe humor in blanket fashion, but caseworker culture and experience tend to prescribe it as a remedy to burnout. Nora (an intake caseworker for 7 months and a treatment caseworker for over 4 years) was asked how she manages this tension. She replied, "I think they [social work educators] preach a lot about trauma informed care" and "if that happened to you like how would you react or like if someone was making fun of you for something that happened, like how would you feel?" She was then asked to answer that question. She replied,

> I would feel bad . . . I've already been through this horrific event and now you're making fun of me for it behind my back. Like even if like that happened with your friends, like, let alone professionals that were supposed to be like working with you and supporting you. I feel like that so like . . . I don't know, I just would feel I don't want to say violated but like it just [would] make me feel even worse about myself."

After Nora was asked about her experiences with humor in the field, the tension came into full light when she stated that she "definitely" utilizes this type of humor on a regular basis, and felt it is an "automatic response" for managing her negative emotions and stress. Nora noted her feelings of "guilt associated with it."

Similarly with Christy, this "guilt associated" with using humor in the field caused her to struggle to make sense of how her humor fits with her professional ethics as a caseworker. She describes her use of humor as a way to deal with her "trauma" and "sadness." She would take an optimistic orientation in investigating referrals in the hope that the allegations of abuse and neglect she was looking into were not true. In the cases where they were true, and sometimes horrifically so, it "hit" her "like a ton of bricks." So, using humor while conducting investigations in the field made them "just a little bit easier to kind of like, kind of laugh it off . . . and cope with the situation." However, she mentioned "ethically, you know, I don't know what that says about me." She worried her humor could "be considered unethical" yet she does not think that she has a "mean bone in her body nor a mean bone in any [caseworker] that was joking around" with her. As she freely talked through this dilemma in her interview, she tried to reconcile how a sense humor helped her but misaligned ethical standards as a professional. While doing so the strain from her internal conflict was palpable.

Mandy (intake caseworker for 5½ years and a treatment caseworker for 6 months) also stated a sense of doing something wrong by using humor. Mandy jokingly reported how she used humor with colleagues when "going into a meth lab," about clients that do odd things because of their "mental health," and about the behavior of clients under the influence of drugs. She reported these observations of unsafe situations "can be twisted" in their retelling into "comical things." During her interview, she seemed to be enjoying recalling her memories of these events as humorous but then would say that her humor about it was "wrong." When she was asked to elaborate, she stated:

> Because normal people wouldn't see [humor in this] as appropriate. They would take it as me being demeaning or as just inappropriate because they don't understand. In my opinion, they don't understand the traumas that we are exposed to. Thus, we deal with it [through] laughter and humor.

When asked if she felt the use of humor was wrong, Mandy stated,

> It depends . . . if it's someone else that understands me, no, it's not wrong . . . if I go home and I tell my mom this joke about someone, then yeah, it's wrong because she doesn't understand. She's never been in human resources, let alone child welfare. She wouldn't find it funny that I went to a meth lab and the guy came after me with a knife. You know, where me and my colleagues were like, bucket list goals done!

For Mandy, the ethics behind the humor is okay, but only around other caseworkers and done to manage negative emotions and stressors. It is the maintenance of the appearance of professionalism in the eye of those outside of the organization which would make the use of humor a breach of ethics.

Similarly, Gina (intake caseworker, in social services for 25 years) expressed concerns about people outside of the agency hearing the type of humor she and her coworkers share. She said, "you have to be very careful about who could hear you if you're going to use dark humor." She elaborated on this concern by stating,

[At the office]you're in cubicles and you're in close quarters. You might be on the phone with a parent of a child who's been seriously victimized and . . . for that parent to hear the laughter going on in the background is awful to me. I never liked that. I would try to take sensitive phone calls on a mobile phone in another room just because I knew that laughter was going to come. Anytime there's a cluster of people, you're going to hear the laughing and in some situations, you didn't want to deal with that laughter in the background when you were on the phone. Um that to me was a big negative, like, I know, like, we need to do this. I'm guilty of it myself, I might be over there with a group laugh[ing] and not realizing somebody is on the phone or forgetting that somebody is on the phone. So yeah, I think that was kind of a negative part of it . . . be careful in who hears you. . . . I mean, you've got those calls back to the supervisor saying hey, um, . . . I overheard a caseworker saying this to somebody else. And it was a crude joke.

Gina concluded by connecting humor directly to breaches of professionalism. She stated that it is important for caseworkers to know who is within earshot and to be "careful" about what "comes out of your mouth" because it "could be heard by others and you always should be aware of that as a professional."

Rose (an intake caseworker for 16 years and a general caseworker for 3 years) also expressed that humor could impact people's perception. For example, she was out on a case once and she needed the birth mother to come home right away to get her child. The birth mother was not coming home from work as fast as Rose would have liked her to. Rose needed to address safety concerns about the birth mother's children and Rose was frustrated that the birth mother was not coming to get her children, so she used humor. At a later date, Rose stepped back from the situation and thought about what occurred. The day she was addressing the case, she did not even think about the fact that the birth mother did not want to leave work because she needed a job and income to care for her family. Rose's frustration and then humor had her lose sight of other issues that could be occurring within the case. Rose went on to mention, "I think in that respect" "sometimes humor can kind of gloss over those pieces and the challenges," which can be a negative impact of humor, even though it is not the "intention." This could be problematic for the organization because caseworkers could "lose sight of their mission" and be "disrespectful" towards clients, even "though the intent behind it" is not meant to be harmful, it could be an issue.

There could also be concerns noted that humor is offensive and problematic to others. Toni (treatment caseworker, 10 years) provided an example of humor that went too far. She had a coworker that used a racist statement, that came off like she was better than the other person (superiority theory of humor). For her coworker, it was funny, but Toni felt that this was "inappropriate" and this type of humor, for Toni, was viewed as "detrimental." She explained that "as a social worker" "when I see other people who have their degrees in social work" and they laugh about race it upsets her. She feels like as a social worker you are "supposed to be fighting racial . . . injustices." For her, she does not like "humor about race" and that is the only humor that she is not okay with. However, she does acknowledge that sometimes her humor might not be perceived well by others either. The joke about race, she felt was inappropriate and it needed to be "addressed," especially if workers are saying things like this to clients that could offend them.

Offending others can cause caseworkers concerns about perception of their humor as challenging ethics leading to disciplinary action by management. For instance, Steven (intake caseworker, 11 months) expressed concerns about possibly being turned into the "ethics committee," being "written up," or even being "fired" for using ill-timed or inappropriate humor. The concerns caseworkers have about humor being unprofessional, unethical, and being disciplined for their use of humor impacts caseworkers and the organization, especially when it is a wide-spread and regularly used technique to diffuse stress and reduce negative emotion.

As previously mentioned, due to the contradictions between education, formal work ethics, and the informal shared culture of social work, caseworkers have internal conflict about the use of humor they must balance. On one end, they feel like using humor is wrong, problematic, offensive, unprofessional, and unethical. On the other end they feel like they need to use humor to manage emotions and stress. They find it is a way to build trust, reduce stress, and collectively prevent burnout. This becomes a balancing act for caseworkers and causes internal conflict. Missing in this balance is the fact that most agency leaders neglect to address how humor should be used in the workplace, beside falling back on blanket statements regarding ethics. They do not have any formal guidelines on appropriate humor and rarely provide clarity on what is inside and outside of professional boundaries. As such, caseworkers burn time, energy, and efforts over being concerned about being disciplined for their humor and monitoring their humor without clarity of what is appropriate. This causes a different form of stress for them.

SUMMARY

Since humor has positive effects of managing emotions and stress, building group cohesion, helping with workflow and negative impacts of monitoring and challenging professionalism and ethics it needs to be addressed at the systemic level. In the next chapter we explore the differences between how intake and treatment departments use humor to manage their negative emotions and stress. Which answers our final research question: Are there any similarities and/or differences in how intake and treatment employees utilize humor?

Chapter 6

The Battle of the Caseworkers

We found that there are both similarities and differences between how case-workers in intake and treatment departments utilize humor. Humor is used among caseworkers in both departments to mitigate negative emotions such as fear and sadness, reduce stress, and manage nervous discomfort. Yet there are also clear differences between the two departments regarding caseworker humor. We found one clear difference is how intake department caseworkers use darker humor than treatment caseworkers. We also found that this was due, in part, to the ability for treatment caseworkers to use humor with their clients far more often than intake caseworkers. In this chapter, we first review the similarities in the two departments, then we will review the differences.

THE ARMOR OF HUMOR

Child welfare caseworkers prepare every day for the war on the crime against the abuse of children. Unlike traditional war, this war's sole mission is to protect children and ensure their safety. Instead of uniforms and weapons they are armed with clip boards and cell phones. However, Ella (intake caseworker for 2½ years) mentioned that they do indeed wear armor too. This "armor" is made out of humor that shields caseworkers from negative emotions and stressors. The "armor" of humor keeps feelings and stressors from "hitting" the caseworker. It also works from within by letting all the "badness" out of the caseworker and assists in changing the "mood" associated with nega-tive feelings and stressors. Without this "armor" of humor, caseworkers like Violet reported that they would be "worse off mentally" and not be able to "move forward" with work. Therefore, humor is needed to manage emotions and stressors related to their employment.

Betty (treatment caseworker, 3 years) mentioned that she thinks this armor of humor is a requirement for the job. She stated,

If we all sat in the office . . . and tried to process everything we have done in the last year, dealt with in the last year. I think a lot of us would probably walk out of there at the end of each day in tears. It's difficult. Nobody likes us, you know, it's not like anyone's like, "Oh, I love my OCYF caseworker. . . . I can't wait to get another OCYF caseworker." We're not appreciated like all the other quote, first responders are. I think even people like the police more than they like OCYF. Um, so I think if you didn't find humor, if you didn't, if you're not able to laugh at yourself or other people or your clients or your kiddos or you know, anything, I just feel like it would just be such like such a pointless job like you would just constantly feel like you were doing absolutely nothing. Like you weren't helping anyone, you were just sitting there writing court summaries and talking about all the terrible things that you've had to do or seen or you know, whatever it may be. So, I think having a sense of humor does help me get through the day. Like if I can laugh with someone, it's easier for me to get in my car and go do my next home visit than it would be if I was just sitting there in my own head.

Violet (intake caseworker for 5 years and treatment caseworker for 1 year) echoed that child welfare caseworkers "see stuff that the average person shouldn't see and that the body is not able to process in a normal way." Both the intake and treatment department caseworkers utilized this armor of humor as a method to manage negative emotions and stressors related to these experiences.

Caseworkers in both departments use their armor of humor to manage emotions, such as stress, nervous discomfort, fear, and feelings of sadness. Christy, who has been employed at the Office of Children, Youth and Families for the last 20 years as both a treatment and intake caseworker, was able to provide an example of how she used the "armor" of humor to address stress. She was working on a "pretty serious sexual abuse case" with a police officer and they were interviewing an alleged perpetrator. During the interview the perpetrator reported the details of the abuse almost verbatim to what appeared in the referral. During his confession, he eagerly told his story while looking directly into Christy's eyes. She and the officer looked at each other in disbelief because the alleged perpetrator "literally leaned forward and almost made like a motion with his like genitalia." She recalled thinking to herself "holy shit." After the perpetrator was arrested and taken away, Christy describes having feelings of wanting to cry and being stressed but instead using lots of humor with the police officer about the situation. The two were laughing about "someone looking through a peephole and masturbating then eagerly showing us or telling us he's doing it." For her, using humor "to make fun of his action or his quirkiness" helped her manage these feelings, as well as push down all the negative emotions stemming from the realization of what "this guy really did to this girl." In short, this armor of humor for Christy is a coping mechanism for stress.

Caseworkers also use the armor of humor to address feelings of discomfort with clients. Jade (a general caseworker for 6 years) did some research on the client's background on a case she had, to prepare before meeting with them. She heard rumors that the mother was a prostitute and that the father "portrayed himself as a macho gangbanger." Jade went onto a local website known for illegal services like prostitution. She recalls finding information about the father including a link to "BigDicksRuS.com" and clicked on the link to find "a picture of your clients dick." Jade showed the picture to her coworkers, and they made jokes about the small size of his penis. More digging by her revealed that he was "pimping himself out" on "gay and bisexual websites" which flew in the face of his portrayal of himself as a masculine heterosexual "gangbanger." In her recall, she said she joked about the size of his penis and his sexual orientation to cope with other emotions and stressors she was feeling about the case. She also stated that this was a way for her to manage the uncomfortable situation of finding this type of personal information out while investigating the client. Caseworkers also use humor to cope with fear.

Child protective workers are at an increased risk of violence from the clients they serve compared to other human service workers (Shin, 2011). To deal with this reality caseworkers sometimes utilize humor to manage their emotions of fear of violence. Novah, a treatment caseworker for 1½ years, was working on a case that she was newly assigned to. She recalled that the visit was not in a "good town," because it is known to have a large number of problems stemming from heroin use. Therefore, the intake caseworker that handled the referral investigation decided to travel to the home with Novah. The house was thought to be a "drug house" so the two joked about the fears they had. She said she was having thoughts like "I don't know what I'm getting myself into here. But hopefully I don't get shot." When the caseworkers were invited into the home, they completed their entire visit while several adults slept—ostensibly under the influence of heroin—on the living room floor. When they got back to their car after the visit, the two started to make jokes about the neighborhood. She recalled joking with her coworker about the experience "well I got myself into this you know. I chose this job, and this is what I'm having to do. . . . I never pictured myself in this situation but, here I am." Novah recalled also saying to her partner in jest, "Wouldn't it be funny if I came here and then I ended up like getting shot on the street or something like that." This dark humor about being shot helped Novah express concerns for her bodily safety while also "help[ing] alleviate" the fears of the "serious situation." She said this allowed her to feel "less scared" by saying what could happen in a humorous way. She recalls sitting there laughing with her coworker just so that everything would be okay. For her, humor aided in her ability to manage those emotions related to fear. Novah expressed that humor is a "coping mechanism" because her job is "serious" and "humor is like a rampant thing to try and just deal with things."

Laughing about being shot, extracting a confession from a perpetrator that mimicked "looking through a peephole masturbating," and encountering "a picture of your client's dick" during a background investigation helped caseworkers manage their negative emotions and stress. Charlotte (intake caseworker for 5 years) expressed that humor does this by "lightening up the situation" and relieving the "pressure" of the work. She went on to state, "like we know it's going to be rough. It's going to be a bad day. But like it just kind of, I think gives you a brief second of relief." Phoebe (intake caseworker for 9 years and treatment caseworker for 1 year) explained that dark humor was a way to "self-regulate" the "deeper emotions." This humor is needed to prevent "breaking down and crying" and letting things bother you "internally."

Whose Humor Is Darker?

In this section we focus on the differences between caseworker humor in the two departments, which has implications when it comes to addressing humor in training and policy procedures. One difference is that most participants in this study claimed that intake caseworkers use darker humor more frequently than treatment caseworkers. They attributed this to the unique situations they are exposed to and the nature of their investigative work. Most participants felt that intake caseworker's job role exposes them to more trauma, and therefore express more "crude" forms of humor. As well as engaging in more controversial topics with humor. However, it is noted that "inner group" norms play a role in the type of humor that is used.

Overall, there seemed to be consensus (34 out of 35) participants that felt that intake caseworkers are exposed to more trauma in their job role. Toni, a treatment caseworker for 10 years, stated that humor is darker and,

> more frequent with intake workers than it is with like the treatment workers because they are going out way more than treatment workers and they're going into homes for the first time, whereas treatment workers are going into homes where intake workers have already been to.

Hazel (a treatment caseworker for 2 years) added that intake caseworkers use "humor a little bit more" than treatment caseworkers because they "see a lot of the really bad things" and they are "the first to respond with the coroner when there are the fatalities." She gave the example of intake caseworkers in her office having to respond to three children falling from an upper floor apartment window, of which two died on impact. She said that intake caseworkers are the "first ones out there with the coroner's office doing the walkthrough." She recalled that her office had two other cases involving deaths that intake workers had to address. One case was an instance of a mother "throwing a baby over a fence and a dog got to it" and the other was "a mother that shot her two children and then herself outside of a store." Hazel explained that in general intake caseworkers "see like the really, really bad things and by the time [the case] gets to [treatment], they've sort of mitigated some of those pretty egregious safety concerns." Therefore, in Hazel's eyes, intake caseworkers have a "more crass sense of humor."

Evelyn, who was mainly an intake caseworker over the course of her career, mentioned that intake caseworkers experience more "trauma because we are the first responders" and that they also "use humor a little bit differently and maybe even more frequently because when the case is transferred to a treatment caseworker, intake has "cleaned it up or made it look pretty" and "the children have been removed from that trauma." Evelyn went on to report that intake caseworkers "certainly use gallows humor more frequently" because of this. Trish (intake caseworker for between 2 and 3 years and a treatment caseworker for 1 year) also explained that "intake humor is completely different than treatment" because intake caseworkers are exposed to types of situations and treatment "never see[s] that part" of the immediate crisis.

Violet, who was mainly an intake caseworker but has experience as a treatment caseworker, also notes that intake caseworkers use darker humor more frequently due to their job role, which makes them "more crude." She said she has been told by some treatment caseworkers that intake casework humor is too "derogatory or offensive" but they do not understand that intake caseworkers are coping with the "full effects that we have during the investigation of listening to a child disclose the sexual abuse or the physical abuse." Christy, who was an intake caseworker for 5 years, noted that intake caseworker's job roles are to be the "first person knocking on the door" from their agency. "You never know what's going to happen" when you catch people off guard.

Naomi worked in both the intake (5 years) and the treatment (3 years) departments, and she mentioned that "treatment was definitely not the same humor . . . it wasn't that dark twisted humor, as it is in intake." However, she attributed the darker content to "intake being such fast paced and with treatment, it's more about getting to know these families." As a treatment caseworker, Naomi does not "feel as comfortable making fun of the families" that she is working with "so closely for so long." She went on to say that when a treatment caseworker has a family they are longer-term clients, "it comes to the point where you don't want that humor to interfere with your work or you don't want to accidentally say something [inappropriate] in front of them."

All but one participant (34 out of 35) felt that intake caseworkers utilized darker humor and attributed the difference to their role as an investigator that exposes them to more traumas, while also stating that the treatment caseworker used less dark humor due to their therapeutic role. As a result, intake caseworkers have a different type of humor that is seen as dark and "crude." In addition, they utilize humor more frequently due to their exposure of consistent traumas. However, "inner group" dynamics can play a role with humor. Therefore, some participants were utilizing the darker humor with the treatment caseworker as well. These findings extend research about humor in relation to stress and the sociology of emotions and add more nuance to the implications it has at the organizational level. Another difference among intake and treatment caseworkers, because of their job roles, is treatment caseworkers have the ability to use humor with clients.

HUMOR WITH CLIENTS

The participants in our interview study stated that treatment caseworkers use humor more effectively with their clients, which is also due to the uniqueness of their job role. One day at work Nora, a treatment caseworker, who was headed out to her client's house called out to her office mate, "okay Charlottee, I am heading out to save lives!" Charlotte, an intake worker, who was also about to leave the office replied, "Bye Nora, I am heading out to go ruin lives!" This exchange reveals how intake and treatment caseworkers view the core of their work, and in turn, their ability to utilize humor with their clients. Since treatment caseworkers have more of a therapeutic relationship with clients and are out to "save lives" they are able to build the type of rapport needed to use humor more freely with clients.

Isabella, an intake caseworker for 1½ years, reported that she does "envy" that her treatment coworkers get to use humor with clients, and she could not. She acknowledged that the nature of her work investigating allegations in a referral make clients see her as there to "take their children." Isabella understands that her visits are likely "part of the worst day of their [her clients] life and they're not going to like [her]." She "wish[s] there was a way" that she could use humor in the situation because she thinks it would make her "feel a little more human" and less like a faceless government bureaucrat. Yet she learned the hard way that she could not. Isabella recounted a time she tried to use humor when investigating a mother who was a nurse that was referred for "giving her daughter unprescribed marijuana edibles to treat her anxiety." Isabella recalls that she tried joking with the mother by saying sarcastically, "Oh, well, and do you let your daughter drink for anxiety too?" The mother immediately took offense at the comment.

Isabella also recognized that there is even "less liberty to use humor with the kids" during a referral investigation. She explained that as an intake caseworker you have to interview children and be prepared for the details of your interview with the child, to become testimony in court. This means that what you say to a child will be cross-examined. Isabella elaborated that when it comes to children,

> I have to ask you [the child] questions and establish before we even start talking that you know the difference between truth and a lie. Like, I have to start with all of these really serious questions about knowing the difference between truth and lies and you know the difference between X, Y, and Z to establish their understanding of reality. And you're talking about really serious things. If you were to begin to joke around it could compromise the testimony if you get called into court. And the defense attorney could say like, well, but the kid said that you said this, and you weren't serious about that. So how did they know that . . . you were serious about this abuse when you asked about it later? So, I think humor with children can compromise the validity of what we do. And I think that's something that makes me really sad.

Conversely, Hazel, who works in the treatment department, explained that she will regularly use humor with parents and children to help build rapport. She keeps this type of humor "very light and pretty professional" and never says anything "inappropriate with a family." She recalls making one consistent joke with each new family she works with. She will tell parents that at CYS "we really love kids, but we definitely don't want to keep your kiddo forever." Treatment caseworkers also joke to clients "that intake are actually the bad guys, because they're the ones that removed your kids." They as treatment caseworkers are the good guys that are "going to help you get your kids back." She explained that this type of joking helps "lighten the mood a little bit" and helps her "build a relationship" with her clients.

Quinton (intake caseworker for 1 year and treatment caseworker 6 years), when he was a treatment caseworker, provided a nice example of his ability to use humor with a birth family due to his relationship with them. He worked with a family for years due to concerns for their "dirty house." They had been involved with the agency he worked for on and off for years due to the conditions of their home. As a result, Quinton had to remove the children from the home on more than one occasion. However, during one of his active cases with the family there were allegations of sexual abuse and he ended up needing to go to court with the family. At court during one of the first permanency review hearings Quinton wore a gray shirt with a red tie. It was Christmastime, and he was embracing the colors of the season. At court the birth mother told him that his tie is "the most hideous tie" she has ever seen. He then replied to her "you don't like my tie?" To which the birth mother replied "no, I freakin hate that tie. It looks hideous." So, Quinton started to wear the tie every time he had court with the birth mother. The birth mother would laugh about it and said, "there's that fucking tie again." He explained to her that he wears the tie just for her. Quinton stated that the tie "became this joke" between them that he thinks "on some level it, I don't want to say made us closer." However, when "mom and dad saw" him "they could laugh at least." When it came time to terminate parental rights, Quinton still wore his red tie. As you can imagine the termination of parental rights is a stressful and emotional time for the caseworker and especially the birth parents and child. However, they were able to still use humor together. The birth mother commented "I see you're still wearing that tie." Quinton then replied I "didn't feel right to wear any other tie." Quinton noted that this lighted the mood "as much as it could" for a termination hearing.

Treatment caseworkers also use humor with the children on their caseloads. Trish (intake caseworker for between 2 and 3 years and a treatment caseworker for 1 year) mentioned that she uses humor a lot with the kids she works with to make them feel comfortable. Dana (treatment caseworker for 7½ years) also mentioned she uses humor with kids, specifically teenagers. She makes "a lot of jokes" and "most of them seem to land." She keeps the humor "light" with her clients especially when she feels "pretty welcome in people's homes." She makes it a "point to remember little things about their lives" and use humor to "make it known" that she cares about their lives and their family. Dana states, "you're kind of a big part of it for at least, you know, six months to a year and . . . I've had cases for literally four years." Dana went on to describe one time she used humor to counsel an adolescent minor who was using marijuana and smoking cigarettes. As part of her treatment plan, Dana was required to provide informational lessons about legal aspects of drug and nicotine use for minors even though the client would be turning eighteen next month. She joked with the client about how some of the lessons were going to be moot very soon. During the lesson she also allowed her client to use the sarcastically reply "Okay, Mom!" to her cautions. These examples show that treatment caseworkers' job roles and interactions with clients allow for more flexibility to use humor. Treatment caseworkers use humor to ease negative emotions and dictate aspects of the therapeutic relationship with clients. Organizational leaders should be aware of the value humor brings to the therapeutic relationship as it certainly has implications for treatment caseworker training.

As previously mentioned, caseworkers in both departments use humor to cope with their stress and to manage their emotions but differences in how they use it emerge due to the uniqueness of their job roles. Intake caseworkers utilize darker humor overall and keep it among themselves. Treatment caseworkers use lighter humor and have the ability to use it more often directly with their clients. In the next section, we review an interesting finding about how child welfare organizations respond to caseworker humor. It varies based on the size of the agency.

ORGANIZATIONAL PATTERNS

Although we have already discussed the data that applied to our three original research questions, we thought it was important to add that we found child welfare organizations respond to humor differently depending on their overall size of staffing. Organizational leaders in Children and Youth Services regularly attempt to aid their staff in managing stress and emotions. This includes providing programming, therapists, and safe places to relax. However, these tools often do not formally incorporate humor—especially the types reviewed so far. Regarding humor, Children and Youth Service organizations in this study utilize both permissive and restrictive management methods. In general, beyond unevenly enforced blanket policies condemning the use of humor, CYS agencies have lacked clear communication and direction about humor. As previously hinted at, this has led to lots of confusion among case-workers, which can result in negative impacts to caseworkers, clients, and the agency mission.

Caseworkers experience dilemmas in their work that produce negative emotions and stressors, which they struggle to manage. Some Children Youth and Families offices provide caseworkers with therapists, especially when caseworker have particularly difficult cases that involve the death of a child. Some agencies, such as Christy's, have hired their own in-house therapist to work with caseworkers on a routine basis. Despite recognizing the proactive approach to promoting well-being from management as positive, Christy mentioned that this solution has its drawbacks because of the flooding of work,

> You can't schedule [a therapy session] when you know something so sad is going to happen. If it's not the right day and the therapist is not there, in child welfare like one bad day, it's like five years it seems like, you know. Then you forget to schedule and by the next day, like you, you're off to talking about something else and what happened yesterday gets stuffed down. You know, you might not even be able to think straight and then something else is going on and, you know, you're off to court or something. It's just so fast paced that sometimes even just remembering what made you so sad, you know, and I think sometimes, we're like kind of ridiculously funny because we're tired, stressed. We're tired. You know, I think it's a way to kind of almost like keep, you know, to keep going just to keep, like the almost like, some days you're kind of like manic because you . . . you can't, it's fast, you can't, you know, concentrate,

you know, with phones ringing and people yelling and, you know, it's just a stressful environment.

As a result of the fast paced and stressful environment that compounds trauma, caseworkers like Christy end up not using the therapeutic services that their agency provides.

Phoebe (intake caseworker for 9 years and treatment caseworker for 1 year) stated that her agency created a "safe haven" at her office. She was a part of a trauma committee that created a room. They called the room "The Haven." In the room there were coloring books, a salt rock lamp, relaxing music, a bean-bag chair, a yoga mat, and other items to do breathing techniques with. The room was designed to allow caseworkers to go in when they were "stressed out." When asked if she thinks that this helped caseworkers, Phoebe flatly answered "No." She went on to say that these initiatives sound like a great idea but is not something that caseworkers could use instantly when they were in the field or even at the office due to not having time to use them.

Our participants noted that seemingly none of the initiatives that Office and Children Youth and Families formally have in place instantly address their needs to reduce negative emotions and stress the same way as humor. It makes our findings apparent for why caseworkers use it so abundantly.

Permissive and Restrictive Approaches to Addressing Humor

Kelly, who has experience as an intake caseworker for 5 years and a treatment caseworker for 3 years, has experience working at a "big agency" and "a smaller one." At the smaller agency she noted that it feels more like a family, everyone knows each other's cases and the intake and treatment department work well together. She went on to explain that at the smaller office they had "staffing meetings where everyone, intake and ongoing, goes over all of our cases with everybody every week." This way "everyone knows what's going on all the time." Since everyone knows each other's cases and the issues they are dealing with, then in a way, they are exposed to the same dilemmas as others. However, when she worked at the larger agency, she felt like there was this "huge divide" between the intake and treatment department caseworkers. Also, in the larger agency, she only had a staff meeting about her own cases with her direct supervisor. Therefore, she did not know about other casework-er's cases and did not feel as open with everyone. Kelly elaborated that at the smaller office she felt like all the caseworkers are "internalizing it all [at] the same time" and they are all "kind of experiencing what everybody's expe-riencing." She feels like this fact, in the smaller office, brings caseworkers closer, builds trust, decreases the need for monitoring humor and provides them with the ability to use humor more freely with one another.

Kelly mentioned that the larger agency impeded her ability to use humor, although there was no formal policy about the use of humor. At one point the larger agency allowed caseworkers to post humor, however one day administration became strict about the posts in the office. She thinks this was due to the fact administration allowed employees to have their own children in the office. She recalls that the office went to a "100% confidential" with strict rules. New rules were not always consistent or clear and she feels that this was a contributing factor to the larger organization's inability to maintain employees. This is one reason she left the larger agency. "She went on to explain that a job as a child welfare caseworker has "high stress" and the office provides a place to deal with their emotions and stress. If there are so many restrictions on the use of humor in the office this creates a more stressful work environment. These restrictions made caseworkers "afraid to talk or say anything" and she feels this impacts caseworker retention. Unlike the larger office she worked for, the smaller agency viewed their office as a "safety zone" where they were more permissive to use humor as they pleased. Kelly mentioned they joked "in the office, I mean, we joke around about our families or relationships, honestly clients. We have kind of a different sense of humor that you wouldn't use anywhere else." This humor consisted of jokes, comments, deadpan humor, and pranks and occurred freely throughout the office. This also consisted of shooting confetti guns at other employees and playing pranks with the anatomical dolls. In general, the smaller agency she worked for was permissive with their humor and the larger agency was more restrictive. This is one of the reasons she quit the larger agency and now works for the smaller agency. Kelly mentioned, "it makes a big difference when you can use humor and not be stressed out while you're in the office as well as out of the office."

If you recall Jewel's story about the coworker at their office calling the intern and making a fake referral. The coworker was actually a supervisor, which demonstrates that at times not only were caseworkers using humor, so was management. If you recall, the prank did go wrong and the intern started to become upset and was "traumatized" over the prank, which is a concern of using humor. However, it is noted that humor occurred at this small office in a permissive manner. Jewel recalls humor occurring more "regularly" than in the larger agency she worked for. She mentioned that there appeared to be more joy for her in the smaller agency. She recalls one time that they put "wrapping paper" over "everyone's stuff" and they just had "fun." She went on to say that everyone in the smaller agency was "like family." She mentioned she "hung out with every single person." She even recalled a time that her "director would sometimes buy me like a six pack of beer, like, probably inappropriate, but whatever." She went on to explain that the environment at the smaller agency was "a small county vibe." Jewel also has experience working for a larger agency, who was more restrictive with humor. Even though there were more restrictions in general at the larger agency she feels that people still used humor at both agencies. However, there was a need to monitor humor more at the larger agency due to concerns of getting in trouble, offending others, and being seen as unprofessional. Christy also noted that humor was more restrictive at the large office she worked for.

Christy, who works at a larger agency, has been there for 20 years, 7 of those years in a caseworker position. She noted that over time the agency has grown in size and the number of caseworkers they employ has increased. She mentioned that "there's not much laughter at our agency anymore." When she started in 1999, she recalls things being different. Humor used to be more freely used. She went on to explain that "I think everyone's so afraid of all getting written up or being politically incorrect." "People tattle on other people if they, you know, take even a little bit of offense to things. And I know, sometimes I am like ohh that was a little bit off color or maybe like really do have to say the F word that many times." However, she realizes "that's how that person is coping with that situation" they are addressing. She went on to describe that she does not hear much laughter anymore and there needs to be more "laughter and some camaraderie." She describes staff at her agency as being "pissed off" and "always [being] offended." In general, employees are worried about getting in trouble for their use of humor, even if it is how they are managing their emotions and stress. Throughout Christy's interview there appeared to be fear of her administration. She was unable to explain or define the rules that her leaders had about humor. She felt stressed about knowing if her actions would get her in trouble or not. She described her office as being a miserable place void of happiness and she would be interested to know if other offices use humor because she would "consider a transfer."

Kelly, Jewel, Christy, and participants in the study, whether they worked for a small or large agency, all demonstrated the fact that there is no clear communication from their leaders at Office of Children, Youth and Families about how or if they should or should not use humor. This approach to managing humor can be subjective and lead to different treatment and repercussions for caseworkers. Lack of clear policy or direction can open the door for leaders to be unethical, treat their caseworkers differently, and create confusion among staff. It creates an environment where caseworkers feel like they are being treated differently or even targeted. The risk is amplified given what we note about the different types of humor from intake and treatment workers. Therefore, we recommend clear communication and even enforcement policy rooted in the real work uses and risks of the use of humor in CYF agency offices.

SUMMARY

Throughout this chapter, we discussed how the research data collected, in this study, answers the research question, Are there any similarities and/or differences in how intake and treatment employees utilize gallows humor? Both departments use humor to manage their negative emotions and stress. However, intake caseworkers use darker humor more frequently and treatment caseworker can use humor with their clients. In addition, some Office of Children, Youth and Families are permissive, and others are more restrictive about their use of humor. However, agencies do not directly address with their staff how humor should be managed. Organizations should focus more on the environment to access unpleasant situations, rather than employee behaviors that are seen as bad (Maslach, 1982, as cited in Farester, 2016). Addressing environmental factors that cause stress and negative emotions and understanding how humor is being used to address them can aid organizational leaders in addressing the problems that child welfare caseworkers experience. Organizational leaders need to directly address humor as a process for managing emotions and stress and develop strategies to fully harness the power of humor, while also addressing the impacts of humor.

Chapter 7

Humor in Motion

In this chapter, we review our findings in relationship to the literature. There are three key points to how this research contributes to literature: 1) Our research reaffirms the literature about humor theory, stress theory in relation to humor, and the sociology of emotions in relation to humor; 2) Our research extends literature by incorporating impacts of humor in relation to stress and emotions at the organizational level; and 3) This research extends policy implications. From this we then discuss five recommendations that we have based on the literature and our findings: 1) Organizational leaders should keep up to date about child welfare culture, sociology of emotions, stress theory, and humor research, in order to be informed of effective ways to manage their organization; 2) Leaders need to assess how humor is being used and what that reveals about how and what is causing caseworkers stress and negative emotions and management can create useful wellness services; 3) The organizational culture needs to be analyzed to implement possible changes to policies, procedures, and rules; 4) Leaders need to assess job roles in relation to job task, emotions, stress, humor, and group dynamics for training purposes; and 5) Leaders need to communicate openly with caseworkers about the use of humor and their expectations.

THEORETICAL CONNECTIONS

Our research reaffirms the literature about humor theory, and how humor relates to stress theory and the sociology of emotions. Our findings about aspects of incongruity theory, relief theory, and a combination of incongruity and relief theory affirm literature about these theories. In addition, data obtained about superiority theory in combination with relief theory was found in this study, which extends research. The findings in this study also affirm literature on how humor relates to stress theory in the areas of exposure to stress, determination of emotion-focused, problem-focused, or avoidance-focused strategies, and coping strategies (individually and as a group). Furthermore, the findings in this study also affirm areas of the sociology of emotions, such as managing emotions (individually and as a group), concepts about culture in the workplace, and in group dynamics that can create conflict.

Theories of Humor

Child welfare caseworkers in this study mainly identified their humor and dark humor as being due to incongruity, relief, or a combination of both incongruity and relief. However, some noted that humor is due to superiority and relief in combination. Therefore, in this section we review each of these theories and the findings associated with them.

Incongruity theories of humor refer to humor that occurs when we predict an outcome that will occur, and another outcome takes place (Kuipers, 2008). A majority of child welfare caseworkers, in this study, identified finding humor due to the incongruent dilemmas they encountered. This consisted of what they thought should occur and the reality of the situation. Thus, they find humor in the differences. The "naughty or nice list" that Christy's office posted spells out incongruity by providing a visual listing. Employees found humor in the dilemmas they faced (concepts on the naughty list) as opposed to what caseworkers thought should occur (concepts on the nice list). This is also evident in comments like Evelyn's, when she asked her coworker "why didn't you just piss on their floor, they do. Like it would not have mattered." This comment finds humor between the idea of a clean home and the deplorable home that they encountered. Incongruent humor brings two contrasting ideas (clean house and dirty house) together to highlight the differences (Altenau, 2010). This finding extends literature about incongruity theory.

Relief theory, which is derived from Sigmund Freud's *Jokes and Their Relation to the Unconscious* (1976), refers to the feeling that comes from laughter and the gratification received. Child welfare caseworkers, in this study enjoyed playing pranks on one another, engaging in games, and using nonverbal humor. These methods were an attempt to change the environment and bring relief from the more intense negative emotions that child welfare workers experience. This is mirrored by caseworkers, like Sabrina, Mandy, Kelly, and Phoebe who used dolls to bring laughter to the office as a form of relief. Freud's research also addresses the impacts of humor among social relationships (as cited in Kuipers, 2008). Using humor as a form of relief can remove the social constraints associated with social requirements (Monro, 1988). Toni mentioned that if she did not make a joke due to dilemmas she encounters at work, then she would have "a lot of anger and tension." According to relief theory this allows individuals, like Toni, to indulge in the expression of these impulses (Monro, 1988) by providing her with the ability to use humor instead of the expression of anger. The findings in this study, about using humor as relief supports literature in this area. Child welfare caseworkers also used aspects of incongruity theory and relief theory.

Freud's work, along with the work of sociologist Herbert Spencer (1981, 1987) demonstrates how humor can be studied by combining aspects of relief and incongruity together (as cited in Kuipers, 2008). For example, a joke could be due to incongruity but also provide the individual with relief. Jade found humor in the incongruity that her client was a "gangbanger" but "pimping himself out" on "gay and bisexual websites." She also found humor in the size of her client's penis and the claim of the size of his penis. Her humor also provided her with relief from some of her fears about meeting the "gangbanger." Jade used both incongruity theory (claim of the size of his penis and his gangbanger status and "pimping himself out") and relief theory (being scared to meet him). These findings reaffirm the literature about relief and incongruity being used in conjunction. This research also extends aspects of superiority and relief being used in combination.

Superiority theory is humor that is experienced due to an individual thinking that they are better or have more power than others and then finding humor at the expense of those seen as less than them (Vogler, 2011). Gina utilized this type of humor with a sex offender that she had to interview. She pictured "dismembering him" as a way to make herself feel more powerful about a situation that was out of her control. One of the overarching themes of the sociology of humor is "humor [at] expense of others" and how it is heavily associated with the "dark side of humor" (Kuipers, 2008, p. 386). This research affirms this component but extends the literature because Gina also noted that this humor was used to find relief from her emotions. This shows the ability for humor to serve both superiority and relief together. Most research that combines types of humor focuses on incongruity and relief being used together. Therefore, this finding suggests more nuance theorizing is needed in humor theory.

This research not only supports areas of humor theory it also affirms literature on how humor relates to stress theory and the sociology of emotions. This study utilized symbolic interactionist and phenomenological approaches. These two approaches state that humor can reframe situations, so they are seen as less serious (Goffman, 1974) and provides a *looking-glass* view of the world around us, distorting our view of reality and ourselves (Zijderveld, 1982). This concept is supported by this research due to the findings that child welfare caseworkers would use humor to distort their reality due to stress related to dilemmas and changing their perception of the emotions that they are experiencing. Remember Jewel provided the example of making jokes about a birth mother's drug addiction. For her, instead of focusing on the stress or negative emotions, the jokes she told were a way to reframe the stress of the perpetual failure of her client's behaviors and the emotions she was experiencing. This reaffirms research, such as Coughlin's (2002) work that reviews that gallows humor is a method to reframe traumatic situations, thus providing them with a means of coping. In the following section we review how the findings affirm humor and stress literature due to the aspect of exposure to stress, coping strategies (individually and as a group). Then we discuss how the findings affirm humor and the sociology of emotions. In the areas of managing emotions (individually and as a group), concepts about culture in the workplace, and in group dynamics that can create conflict.

Humor and Stress Theory

This research affirms areas of literature associated with humor and stress theory. Including the areas of the demand-control-support model, coping strategies, and social supports, all of which are all supported by this study.

Regarding stress theory, Office of Children, Youth and Families employees experience intense stress, which can cause stress reactions and impact the overall well-being of employees and the organization. Since inequalities due to social conditions increase the risk of exposure to stressors (Mirowsky & Ross, 2003; Thoits, 1995), then leaders need to understand how employees all have different preconditioned stressors due to these social conditions. Furthermore, understanding the organizational, demand-control-support model allows organizational leaders to know how preconceived stressors cause chronic and job strain and how it results in emotional reactions. These strains are important to recognize to decrease employee burnout and emotional exhaustion. According to research, if employees are feeling like they have high demands and low decision making this can increase job strain (Karasek, 1979). This research supports this as child welfare caseworkers, in this study, noted that their demands are high, however they have little control over their clients' actions and the dilemmas they face thus creating more stress.

Furthermore, these findings support other areas of stress theory. According to stress theory, coping attempts are typically directed toward the issue itself (problem-focused strategies), the emotional reaction from the issue (emotion-focused strategies) (Thoits, 1995), or an attempt to abstain from the problem and emotions (avoidance-focused strategies) (Endler & Parker, 1994; Folkman & Moskowitz, 2004, as cited in Rowe & Regehr, 2010). Caseworkers in this study have used all these strategies to cope. Isabella used humor with other providers to understand better the problems (problem-focused strategy) that her clients were dealing with and so that she and the provider were interpreting the situation the same. Novah used humor to address the emotion of fear (emotion-focused strategy) and other caseworkers in this study noted they would brush situations off by using humor to avoid (avoidance-focused strategy) the problem and emotions all together. Although caseworkers in this study experienced each of the strategies, many caseworkers focused on their coping as an emotion-focused strategy. According to research, it is important to use problem-focused strategies. However, due to the emotional situations that caseworkers encounter and lack of perceived control of the situation, they are more likely to be using emotion-focused strategies. The lack of control leaves caseworkers to seek out ways to feel like they are in control as a form of coping. The demand-control-support model emphasizes the impacts of control on stress and perceived stressors that result in emotional reactions, which lead to job strain and impact work environment and decisions (Farester, 2016). Humor can be a method for control that reduces stress and job strain and can result in better work decisions. Therefore, it is recommended that leaders assess their employees to understand how they are coping. Research suggests that professionals can use any of these types of coping (problem-, emotion-, and/or avoidance- focused) and in any combination. Reframing the situation through humor can be an attempt individuals use to cope and in return helps individuals, like child welfare caseworkers, focus on the problem at hand. This information further extends research in this area.

Another area of stress theory associated with humor that is supported by this research is the idea that humor is a copy strategy. Humor and stress literature review that humor can be a means for coping with stress, individually. Literature about gallows humor note its use "as a coping strategy by social workers, journalists, police officers, soldiers, and crime scene investigators" (CSIs; Buchanan & Keats, 2011; Riolli & Savicki, 2010; Roth & Vivona, 2010; van Wormer & Boes, 1997; Wright, Powell & Ridge, 2006). This coping strategy is typically used when situations cause distress to an individual (Johnson, 2007) and assists in creating a perception of control. Stress theory reviews the importance of control on decreasing stress (Thoits, 1995). Caseworkers use gallows humor, which has proven effective in providing social control (Obrdlik, 1942), relieving stress (Wright et al., 2006), and is a means to cope with stress. Caseworkers like Trish, Olivia, Rose, Christy, Charlotte, Phoebe, and Gina all expressed their use of humor to cope. This supports the literature that humor is a coping strategy for stress. However, it is important to note that some research is mixed on the effectiveness of humor on reducing stress, such as Coughlin's (2002) study on police officers that found no correlation between gallows humor and lower stress levels. This research refutes that claim.

Literature also reviews that humor can be a method for coping with stress among groups. Since humor is a method for coping with stress (Craun & Bourke, 2015) and stress theory states the importance of social support on decreasing stress (Thoits, 1995), humor among groups can be a method of coping with stress as a group and can build group cohesion and aid in work-flow. This is evident in our findings that affirm research about the social components of coping with stress through humor. As well as humor's ability to help groups function (Obrdlik, 1942). Throughout literature humor has proven effective in bringing groups together in an attempt to manage and share their emotions (Turcotte, 2017), as a way of social control (Obrdlik, 1942) and allows individuals relief due to the fact they can access other supports even if they do not utilize them (Dunkel-Schetter & Bennett, 1990). This in return provides *structural support*, which is linked to the degrees of social isolation and integration (Thoits, 1995).

Humor and the Sociology of Emotions

This study also affirms aspects of literature about humor and the sociology of emotions. Particularly in the areas of humor's ability to manage emotions individually, manage emotions among groups, influence group culture, and create inner group dynamics.

Humor and the sociology of emotions reveal that humor can be a method to manage emotions individually. Child welfare workers utilize what Hochschild (1979) refers to as emotional management, due to emotional labor at work, to address the intense emotions that they experience at work according to a set of rules that society regulates (Hochschild, 1979) and organizational rules. In our findings, caseworkers like Betty utilized humor to manage her emotions due to her employment in accordance with the way she is expected to. Humor allowed her to use humor backstage so she could "move on" with her work tasks and perform her work the way management intends her to. Employees that work in emotionally demanding circumstances can experience burnout and compassion fatigue if those emotions are not managed (West, 2015). Olivia and Mandy expressed that humor could aid in their own ability to continue to do their work and not burn out from employment, which is supported by the literature. Keller (1990) states that gallows humor can occur due to uncertainty and be used to prevent burnout (as cited in Scott, 2007).

Humor and the sociology of emotions also reveal that humor can be a method to manage emotions among groups of people. Gallows humor has proven effective in bringing groups together to manage and share their emotions (Turcotte, 2017) and is a form of social control (Obrdlik, 1942). Humor is also known to be a method to manage the emotions of child protective investigators (Howell, 2008). This research reaffirms that gallows humor is used for managing emotions in groups. This is shown through the pranks and games caseworkers in this research use together. This is solidarity building, through types of humor, that provide a method for bringing caseworkers together, through bonding, and provides them with assistance in managing their emotions.

Another area of literature that this research affirms, about the sociology of emotions and humor, is some of the findings about culture in the workplace. Group culture provides "social solidarity in the functionalist sense" and uses "ingroup humor, repeat jokes, and specific humorous styles and tastes that literally get to define a group, and be used to demarcate its identity" (Kuipers, 2008, p. 379). In our findings, Nora mentioned that she felt that humor was "inappropriate" at first, however she noticed that the culture of her agency used "dark humor" and it eventually became a necessary part of her job. Mandy elaborated on this by saying humor is essential "it's just the culture, the way of the world, the way of that world." The culture, in which a joke is told, determines what is perceived as funny (Scott, 2007). Humor is simply how those in this study define their larger group. Reviewing the topics that make employees laugh and the jokes they tell can help management understand what is bothering caseworkers individually and as a group. This can bring leaders of the agency insight into the possible strengths and weaknesses within the organizations. This extends research about culture in relations to humor among groups.

To further affirm the literature this research notes that those individuals that were not a part of the "in group" using the humor could be offended and feel that humor was unprofessional. If leaders observe the interactions of their employees this will allow them to understand the division among workers that can impact employee self-esteem (Rowe & Regehr, 2010). This can impact the group dynamics in the office and create conflict. The use of dark humor, among groups, can be a signal of what group individuals belong to and have an impact on employee self-esteem (Rowe & Regehr, 2010). Child protective caseworkers can feel a sense of belonging or isolation from certain groups. It is important for leaders to understand these divisions among staff and aid in decreasing them so that they can provide a supportive work environment and meet the organization's mission.

Throughout this section an understanding of these findings affirms the literature about humor theory, and how humor relates to stress theory and the sociology of emotions. Specifically, findings about incongruity theory, relief theory, a combination of incongruity and relief theory, and add nuance to literature about superiority theory in combination with relief theory. These findings also support research around humor and stress theory in regard to aspects of exposure to stress, determination of emotion-focused, problem-focused, or avoidance-focused strategies, coping strategies (individually and as a group). In addition, the findings in this study affirm humor and the sociology of emotions in the areas of managing emotions (individually and as a group), concepts about culture in the workplace, and in group dynamics that can create conflict. In the next section we review how the findings in this study extend literature.

EXTENSION OF THEORETICAL CONCEPTS

Our second main point is that our findings extend literature by incorporating impacts of humor in relation to stress and emotions at the organizational level. Firstly, research typically focuses on stress and humor or the sociology of emotions and humor. There is little theoretical research about child welfare workers that combine humor theory, stress theory, and the sociology of emotions. Therefore, this research extends implications at this level. Secondly, literature mainly focuses on the impacts of humor on the individual or among groups. However, some research talks about the organizational level such as Zijderveld (1982), Davis (1993), and Mulkay (1988), which provide studies that contribute to the research of humor by incorporating micro and macro facets (as cited in Kuipers, 2008). Our research affirms the literature about the impacts of humor at the micro and mezzo level and further extends knowledge at the organizational level (macro). Showing the connection between the individual, groups and shedding light on additional impacts that humor can have on the organization.

As previously noted, there has been little research that combines theories of humor, aspects of the stress process model, and the sociology of emotions. A vast amount of research focuses on humor used to cope with stress or humor used to manage emotions. By combining these theories this research reveals the correlation among them. This sheds light on the fact that humor can be used to reduce stress and manage negative emotions at the same time or be used interchangeably. Mandy, Gina, Betty, Dana, and Christy all expressed how humor was used this way for them. Thus, affirming literature about humor and stress and literature about emotions and humor at the same time. This extends the literature by building a connection between stress theory and the sociology of emotions and how humor is a strategy for addressing both stress and emotions. Stress theory, the sociology of emotions, and humor theory all place emphasis on social supports, the reframing techniques of humor, and the psychological impacts of using humor as a strategy. These similarities show the connections among the theories in relation to humor.

The second point of how this research extends literature is how this study supports some of the literature about the impacts of humor at the micro and mezzo level, while extending certain aspects of knowledge at the organizational level (macro). Literature shows that a positive impact of humor is its ability to promote bonding, create coping strategies, and reduce burnout (Mesmer-Magnus, Glew & Chockalingam, 2012). Our research findings support this by showing positive impacts of humor as providing relief, creating group cohesion, building solidarity, and decreasing burnout. Therefore, this research supports literature about the micro and mezzo impacts of humor. This study also supports literature at the micro and mezzo level in that it reveals that humor can change perception and can be offensive among groups.

Thorson's (1993) research on humor notes that its main use is as a coping strategy; however, it can also be an attempt to remove oneself from reality. This is like our findings about how caseworkers would use humor to brush off the negative emotions and stress as an attempt to alter reality. However, literature and our findings reveal that even though this can aid individuals, dark humor can be interpreted as being offensive to others (Coughlin, 2002). In these areas this research supports literature, however this research also adds more nuance by extending literature on the negative impacts of humor at the micro and mezzo level. It also extends research because it can have implications at the organizational level. Due to humor's ability to offend others, being seen as unprofessional, and challenging social work ethics it has a direct influence on how the organization is viewed.

The findings in this study note that humor can cover up trauma, alter identity, and impede connections with others outside of the organization. This adds new meaning to research on the negative impacts of humor and gallows humor. This can have important implications on how to care for employees. We have shown the connections between impacts of humor on the individual and groups, however we note impacts that can occur at the individual, group, and organization level, which is where we extend the research further.

Throughout these findings it was discovered that individuals and groups of caseworkers use humor to find relief from stress and negative emotions. This in return can show leaders how their employees manage their emotions, stress, and how it relates to their work responsibilities, the effects it has on their organization, and how they can assist their employees. There has been little research that connects humor to decision making by leaders. In this study, Betty mentioned that humor helps her manage emotions and stress and provides her with the ability to complete work tasks. It is important for leaders to understand this as it can have direct implications on work outcomes.

A second way that this study extends research, at the micro, mezzo, and macro levels, is by connecting the individual, group, and organization levels of cohesion. Humor can build group cohesion and solitary, which aids in the ability to ask others for assistance when needed. This in return provides a sense of belonging and understanding of work life and is dependent on whether a caseworker is ready to produce and receive the type of humor that occurs in the organization. This ultimately helps with workflow and decreases burnout, which is key for an organization to meet their mission. This shows the implications that humor can have at the individual and group level that directly influence the organization. Since most Office of Children, Youth and Families has difficulty with maintaining staff and ensuring their staff meet guidelines, humor through group cohesion can be used to build these relationships to ensure workflow and decrease turnover rates. Inability to become a part of the cohesive group is contingent on a worker's ability to use dark humor and could have impacts on the organizations.

A third way that this study extends research at the micro, mezzo, and macro levels, is by connecting the individual, group, and organization levels due to the negative impacts of humor. In this study it was discovered that the negative impacts of humor are that it covers up trauma and alters identity and connections to those outside the organization. There is little research that has yelled this information about the negative impacts of humor, therefore these findings extend the research in this area. However, it is important to note that these impacts can directly impact caseworker's ability to function in their job role. Caseworkers like Sabrina are "dulled" by the job and have lost their "sparkle," which has "ruined" her relationships with others outside of the field. Leaders need to assess if their employees are covering up trauma, struggle with components of identity, or have impaired connections. These impacts are connected to the organization and can have ramification for the mission.

POLICY IMPLICATIONS

This research is an extension of stress theory, the sociology of emotions, and humor in combination and furthers research about organizational concepts such as burnout, socialization, and cohesion. There is little research that connects humor with stress (as coping) and the sociology of emotions (managing emotions) as being a part of work group dynamics (with few exceptions of a small group of researchers) for organizational decision making, policy, and training implications. Within an organization there are norms surrounding emotions, stress, and humor that are impacted by formal and informal procedures. Therefore, understanding emotional labor, stress theory, and how humor plays a role can provide leaders with methods to improve their organization as well as their employee's well-being and effectiveness. In addition, this research extends knowledge of policy implementation and training procedures. Organizations, such as the Office of Children, Youth and Families have a set of defined rules and policies for their staff. These standards can sometimes impose unrealistic expectations for staff and/or interfere with the reality of the job task.

It is important for organizations to understand what the shared emotional norms and emotional techniques are of their employees (Fields et al., 2006). Lois's (2003) book, *Heroic Efforts: The Emotional Culture of Search and*

Rescue Volunteers, reviews research conducted on how employees manage their emotions and the emotions of those that they rescue. It is also noted that employees had their own culture of norms based on handling stress, feelings, deep acting, emotions, and emotional rewards. This is like child welfare workers and their culture about how they are managing their own emotions and those of their clients, as well as how they handle stress. Understanding the belief system associated with the organization and what employee's shared beliefs are can help organizational leaders meet their mission (Fields et al., 2006). Since organizations, such as the Office of Children, Youth and Families, can impact the emotions of employees and inversely, it is important to understand these emotional exchanges. "Job performance, decision making, creativity, turnover, [and] prosocial behavior" (Barsade & Gibson, 2007, p. 36) are all associated with *affect* ("an umbrella term encompassing a broad range of feelings that individuals experience, including *feeling states* and *feeling traits*") (Barsade & Gibson, 2007, p. 37). Organizational cultures can challenge or embrace organizational beliefs; therefore, leaders need to take into consideration emotions that are impacting organizational cultures (Hochschild, 2003; Fields et al., 2006) and take this into consideration when creating policies. One way to understand emotions is through their use of humor since they are using humor as emotional management. This supports the implications for literature and policy about emotional culture and extends how humor can shed light in this area.

Ruchti's (2012) research further expands on the idea that understanding the emotional labor of employees can aid in creating effective policies. Ruchti (2012) researched nurses' emotional management and the emotions of their patients. Their organization had formal policies against forms of harassment due to *intimate conflict.* However, nurses in the study did not utilize these formal procedures. Instead, they would use informal strategies such as confronting, ignoring, or negotiating. Child welfare caseworkers did not typically use formal policies (therapy or "The Haven"). Instead, they informally use humor with their coworkers as a strategy of addressing conflict with their clients and the dilemmas they face. In Ruchti's research, due to this finding, it is mentioned that organizational leaders could utilize strategic decisions to improve their organization. This could also be used in the child welfare system. Understanding these aspects of emotional labor, stress theory, and how humor plays a role can provide leaders with methods to improve their organization as well as their employee's well-being and effectiveness.

This research extends policies about training procedures. Hochschild's (2003) book, *The Managed Heart,* assesses emotional labor among bill collectors and flight attendants. Although both experience emotional labor and utilize the same processes to regulate emotional rules, the flight attendants enhance the status of their customers while bill collectors diminish this status. Hochschild's (2003) found that training was different among flight attendants and bill collectors due to their employee role and how this played a part in emotional management. All Office of Children, Youth and Families employees attend standard training upon employment in the organization. Child protective caseworkers' task consists of determining abuse (intake department) and therapeutic aspects of helping families resolve those issues (treatment department). Our findings note that due to the different job roles, miscommunication or conflict has the potential to occur and monitoring humor around other child welfare caseworkers is needed. Most of the Office of Children, Youth and Families have the same mission, expectations, and training for both departments. However, since participants noted experiencing different emotions and stressors, different emotions from their clients depending on their job role, and the utilization of humor similarly and differently, then this has implications on how employees should be trained and educated about their job role. This extends the implications for training and furthers policy research. There is no research that we have found that looks at differences and similarities in intake and treatment caseworkers and how this has implications for training procedures.

Organizations, such as the Office of Children, Youth and Families have a set of defined rules and policies for their staff. These expectations can sometimes impose unrealistic standards of staff and/or interfere with the reality of a job task. Humor is an action that takes place that can bridge the gap between the individuals and the organization. Leaders can utilize an understanding of humor as a way to close this gap by meeting caseworkers where they are rather than placing unrealistic expectations and policies on them. This understanding can help create training, rules, and policies that reflect the reality of field work, dilemmas, and the way that caseworkers experience stress, emotions, and humor. Therefore, humor should be allowed to operate in the organization and leadership needs to take advantage of the benefits of this knowledge and maximize the positives and minimize the negative.

RECOMMENDATIONS

Based on empirical research and the findings of this study we have five recommendations. Firstly, organizational leaders should keep up to date about child welfare culture, sociology of emotions, stress theory, and humor research, in order to be informed of effective ways to manage their organization. Secondly, leaders need to access how humor is being used and what that reveals about how and what is causing caseworker's stress and negative emotions so management can create wellness services for employees. Thirdly, the organizational culture needs to be analyzed to implement possible changes to policies, procedures, and rules. Fourthly, leaders need to assess job roles in relation to job task, emotions, stress, humor, and group dynamics for training purposes. Fifthly, after observing staff and assessing the culture to implement wellness activities, training, and policies, organizational leaders could benefit from communicating findings with staff. These recommendations will help organizational leaders directly address humor as a process for managing emotions and stress. It also provides leaders with strategies for fully harnessing the impacts of humor and understanding their staff, group dynamics, and the impacts of their policies. All of which contribute to the outcomes of their organization's mission.

The first recommendation is that organizational leaders keep abreast of research about child welfare culture, sociology of emotions, stress theory, and humor so they are informed about effective ways to manage their organization. The sociology of emotions can inform leaders about concepts such as emotional labor and techniques they can use to aid their employees. Sociological research can also show leaders that social supports are important with individuals (micro level) as well as with social systems (mezzo and macro levels). Stress theory provides leaders with an understanding that employees do not show up to work with the same distress. Understanding these differences can help organizational leaders make decisions or at least provide an awareness of stress among different employees individually and as groups (Mirowsky & Ross, 2003). Concepts such as *random* and *systemic stressors*, the organizational, demand-control-support model, chronic strain and how it connects to emotional reactions, emotional exhaustion, and burnout can all aid in ensuring a thriving organization. Furthermore, understanding how and why humor is used is also essential. This allows leaders an understanding of what stressors and emotions staff are experiencing, as well as other implications it has for their organization. Research also reveals that gallows humor at the expense of a victim can be viewed as a signal that an employee lacks compassion and cannot perform quality work (Rowe & Regehr, 2010; as cited in Craun & Bourke, 2014). This can have consequences on the quality of services that the employee and ultimately the organization provides to families. In our findings, it was noted that humor was used about children that were seen as the source of the referral, not the victim. For example, humor was found in the dilemmas that incorrigible teenagers placed themselves or the caseworker in. This type of information is important to know to understand why staff are making comments about incorrigible teenagers and if it has any implications on their empathy and the organization. It is information like this that can help serve clients and the agency's mission more effectively.

Our second recommendation is for organizational leaders to create and implement appropriate wellness programs for managing stress and emotions.

"The most dynamic leader is one who can get a job done while understanding those whom she [he, they] leads" (Steele, 1999, p. 100). Assessing how humor is being used and what that reveals about how and what is causing a caseworker's stress and negative emotions can shed light on underlying issues so that more informed decisions can be made. Throughout this research caseworkers acknowledged that their dilemmas cause stress and negative emotions. They also noted that scheduled therapy and "Safe Haven" rooms were not very effective in meeting their immediate needs of releasing stress and managing negative emotions. This would require leaders to observe staff as well as interview them for feedback about more effective methods, such as using humor. Utilizing this information, along with research, can aid leaders in creating needed wellness services to decrease stress and negative emotions for their caseworkers.

The third recommendation is that the organizational culture be analyzed to implement possible changes to policies, procedures, and rules. "There is always an atmosphere of structure, rules, and hence, expectations for actions. When humans interact, they often rely on the structure that is already present" (Steele, 1999, p. 24). Therefore, leaders need to analyze if their current structure is helpful or impedes the organization's mission. "Culture is within us as individuals, but it evolves as we join and create new groups; the concept of culture is an abstraction, but behavioral and attitudinal consequences are real" (Schein, 2004, p. 351). Therefore, leaders need to observe how caseworkers are using humor and what the emotional norms, emotional exchanges, and techniques are. This can show if an organization's formal and informal policies, procedures, and rules are impacting employees and the mission negatively.

According to Heifetz (1998), leaders need to take steps to guide them with adaptive challenges (such as dilemmas caseworkers encounter). Heifetz's (1998) reviews that a leader must get on the balcony, identify the adaptive challenge (dilemmas child welfare caseworkers are having), keep levels of distress at a tolerable level, focus attention on the issue at hand, give the work back to the people, and protect the voices of all stakeholders. Getting on the balcony refers to looking at the whole organization to get a holistic view of what is going on so that the other steps can be taken. An organization can influence an individual's role taking and emotional management, therefore, leaders within an organization need to understand emotions in their workplace. Fields et al. (2006) discusses that unjust organizations can create unjust emotion work and can enforce stigma and when social order is "unjust or an oppressive one" "monitoring" "helps to maintain social inequalities" (Fields et al., 2006, p. 159). If leaders assess and observe their organizations then they can make needed changes to existing policies that are, oppressing or not effective and then implement policies that help caseworkers with their dilemmas.

Our fourth recommendation is about training. Leaders can implement training on the impacts of job roles, in relation to humor, emotions and stress. Macduff (2005) explains that the benefits of training are that it "establishes a minimum level of competency" and understanding (p. 703). The findings in this study suggest that, due to job roles, there can be a lack of understanding of how and why others are using humor. Currently, in Pennsylvania, core training focuses on job tasks, but does not fully address the difference in the two departments. Current training also does not fully train staff on how to manage emotions, cope with stress, and what the realities of the culture of child welfare are. Training that considers job roles in relation to job tasks, the emotions that each job role can produce from their clients, staff emotions, stress, humor, and group dynamics deepens the level of understanding about these topics among staff. This prepares caseworkers for the reality of the field and produces understanding among departments and could decrease possible conflicts and decrease monitoring of humor backstage, due to lack of understanding about the type of humor being used. Training courses that include these aspects will better prepare new staff and aid current staff.

The fifth recommendation is that leaders communicate with their child welfare caseworkers. After observing staff and assessing the culture to implement wellness activities, training, and making policies, organizational leaders could benefit from communicating with staff about humor, emotions, and stress. Since there is a "reality for person A [the intake department], the reality for person B [the treatment department], and finally and importantly, a shared reality of A and B [child welfare caseworkers]" (Steele et al., 1999, p. 24) communication is needed. This can develop empathy and understanding among child welfare caseworkers. This can also assist leaders, through humble consulting, by obtaining trusting relationships (grounded in shared values and culture) through curious questions and relationships grounded in common work that forms a deeper level of openness, which can help leaders understand more about adaptive challenges (dilemmas). This includes communicating about the impacts of humor at their specific organization, as well as the reason for the implementation of wellness activities, training, and policies. In addition, leaders can encourage healthy ways to utilize humor and attempt to decrease some of the negative components of humor, including expectations for when it is proper to use humor and when it can negatively impact the agency and clients. Communicating openly with caseworkers about the use of humor can help caseworkers feel supported. Research suggests that child welfare employees need social support to become successful at managing their stress and emotions associated with their employment (Conrad and Kellar-Guenther, 2006). This communication can show child

welfare caseworkers that leaders are supportive of them. Since individuals
make attempts to maintain their emotions by using norms as a way to assess
what is expected of them (Fields et al., 2006) this communication is key for
staff and the organization. It also decreases the likelihood of what Thoits
(1989) refers to as *emotional deviance.*

CONCLUSION

Office of Children, Youth and Families employees regularly experience
intense emotions and stressors related to their employment. They are at an
increased risk of violence (Shin, 2011), deal with a number of dilemmas, and
can be emotionally shocked by the situations and details of abuse (Taris &
Schreurs, 2009) and experience anger, depression, uneasiness, guilt, loneliness, helplessness and disappointment in their work (Howell, 2008). As a
result, employees manage their own emotions and feelings while they assist
families, and depending on how they do this, the quality of services to families potentially suffer (Heverling, 2011). There can also be miscommunication among intake and treatment caseworkers due to their job roles. All these
experiences and factors contribute to stress and impact employee emotions.
As a result, child welfare caseworkers utilize negative and positive coping
mechanisms to address stress and emotions related to work duties (Farester,
2016; Heverling, 2011). These coping mechanisms not only help Office of
Children, Youth and Families employees manage their experiences but has
direct impacts on the organization. Child welfare employees need social support and need to process traumatic events that occur daily to become successful at managing their stress and emotions associated with their employment
(Conrad & Kellar-Guenther, 2006). Therefore, it is imperative that organizational leaders understand how employees experience stress and emotions
in the workplace. One way that leaders can understand this is through the
use of humor.

   The purpose of this study was to explore how humor and gallows humor is
used within the Office of Children, Youth and Families and what that reveals
about how employees experience stress and manage their emotions. We used
a qualitative research design that includes a phenomenological analysis and
symbolic interaction frameworks. The following research questions guided
this study: 1) How do Office of Children, Youth and Families employees
(intake and treatment) experience humor and gallows humor, and what does
that reveal about how they are managing stress and emotions related to their
employment? 2) What are the negative and positive effects of the use of gallows humor among individuals, groups, and the organization? 3) Are there

any similarities and/or differences in how intake and treatment employees utilize gallows humor?

The findings show that Office of Children, Youth and Families employees are exposed to a high degree of emotional situations and stressors that revolve around dilemmas. As a result, caseworkers utilize humor as a method to manage these dilemmas. In chapter 4, we discussed the individual components of humor and how the research data collected showed that child welfare caseworkers experience gallows humor and humor concerning dilemmas they encounter. Humor and gallows humor provided a way for employees to cope with stress and the negative emotions they experience due to dilemmas. Employees used strategies, such as sarcastic humor, humor through pranks, juvenile humor, nonverbal humor, and humor that caseworkers use in their mind as methods for managing. These types of humor helped employees find relief from stress and negative emotions as well as provided them with the ability to brush off negative emotions and stress created by the dilemmas they experience. However, humor also covers up trauma, alters identity and disconnects child welfare caseworkers from those that are not employed in the profession.

In chapters 5 and 6, we reviewed humor at the group and organizational level. The intake and treatment departments have similarities due to their use of humor as a means to manage emotions and stress. However, there were some key differences in that the intake department uses darker humor more frequently and the treatment department has the ability to use humor with their clients. Humor not only impacts the group dynamics at the organization, but it also produces some positive and negative outcomes for the organization. Humor supports group cohesion and collaboration and helps workflow to prevent burnout. However, it is something that caseworkers have to monitor around others and humor can be seen as being unprofessional and something that could challenge ethics. The Office of Children, Youth and Families in this study were both permissive and restrictive in their use of humor, however leaders did not directly address with their staff how humor should be managed.

The findings provided an overall picture of how humor is managed by the individual, group and at the organizational level. Understanding how employees individually and as a group manage emotions and stressors can reveal deficiencies and strengths of the employee and organization. It is apparent that they are abundantly using humor and organizational leaders do not have a formal method to manage this. As we have mentioned, the Office of Children, Youth and Families in this study do not directly address with their staff how humor should be managed or acknowledge its impacts. Therefore, leaders are not fully harnessing the power of humor to aid in the wellness of their employees, groups of employees, and the organization itself.

The findings reveal that Office of Children, Youth and Families employees are exposed to emotional situations and stressors that revolve around neglect and the physical and sexual abuse of children. This supports the literature about the stress child welfare workers experience. However, research on the use of humor has just recently started to incorporate the study of humor and the sociology of emotions. This study extends this aspect of research by incorporating the stress process model and humor (which has been recently studied) along with the sociology of emotions. In addition, this study furthers research on the sociology of emotions because it assesses the use of humor between two job roles within the same organizations and its impacts on group dynamics.

Our findings connect humor at the individual, group, and organizational levels. Firstly, the finding connects humor theory, stress theory, and the sociology of emotions. This sheds light on the fact that humor can be used to reduce stress and manage negative emotions at the same time or be used interchangeably. Secondly, this research affirms the literature about the impacts of humor at the micro, mezzo, and further extends knowledge at the organizational level (macro). Since humor can be seen as unprofessional, and challenging social work ethics it can have a direct influence on how the organization is viewed by others. Furthermore, the findings in this study show humor can impede connections with others outside of the organization. All of which have direct impacts on the organizations. This can provide important information for leaders and influence their expectations, rules, and policies. Since individuals, groups, and the organization are all impacted by humor and there are connections at the micro, mezzo, and macro levels and an under-standing of how humor is being used is needed.

This research reaffirms the literature about humor theory, stress theory in relation to humor, and the sociology of emotions in relation to humor. This study also extends literature by focusing on the impacts of humor in relation to stress and emotions at the organizational level and the policy implications that can be made. Therefore, it is recommended that leadership keep current on their education about these areas. It is also recommended that leaders assess how humor is being used in general and what that reveals about how and what is causing caseworkers stress and negative emotions to imple-ment wellness programs. Furthermore, an assessment of emotional norms, emotional exchanges, and techniques (culture) should take place to analyze if the organization's formal and informal policies, procedures, and rules are impacting employees and the mission negatively so needed changes can be made. This includes leaders examining job roles in relation to job task, emo-tions, stress, humor, and group dynamics so proper training for employees can be created. It is further recommended that leaders communicate openly with caseworkers about the use of humor to minimize conflict and judgment and provide understanding, including expectations for when it is proper to use humor and when it can negatively impact the agency and clients. These recommendations based on literature and the findings in this study can help leaders understand how they can fully harness the power of humor and minimize the negative components.

Child welfare caseworkers show up to work with their armor of humor on. They are prepared to serve the sovereign community like any good knight would do. They may not be protecting the king and queen, but they are protecting the children and the community. Their job is a noble one. However, they are not always perceived in a heroic way. But they are. Steal swords are not pointed at them, but the mean words of those that judge them cut just as deep. They go out into the community, just as any knight would venture across the land. Along the way caseworkers find themselves in dilemmas. So, it is imperative that they have their armor of humor. How else are they supposed to get through a normal day at work when, stepping around brain matter, dodging possible harm, finding poop on beds, seeing their client's penis, and getting stuck in the back of a police car?

Methodological Appendix

RESEARCH DESIGN

Qualitative methods were implemented to understand the following research questions: 1) How do Office of Children, Youth and Families employees (intake and treatment) experience humor and gallows humor, and what does that reveal about how they are managing stress and emotions related to their employment? 2) What are the negative and positive effects of the use of gallows humor among individuals, groups, and the organization? 3) Are there any similarities and/or differences in how intake and treatment employees utilize gallows humor? We used a social constructivist lens throughout this study, which told us "how the people in this setting construct their reality" (Patton, 2015, p. 98). Qualitative research examines "the stories of individuals to capture and understand their perspective" (Patton, 2015, p. 8). A qualitative approach was appropriate for the research questions in this study because we were concerned with understanding how people that have been or are currently employed by the Office of Children, Youth and Families experience humor and gallows humor. For this study, we assumed that people all have different realities. We used a combination of qualitative inquiry frameworks to understand the research questions in this study, specifically, phenomenological analysis, heuristic inquiry, and symbolic interaction.

The phenomenological analysis focuses its attention on how people experience a phenomenon and seeks to understand the nature of lived experiences from an individual's view (Patton, 2015). This approach assumes an "essence of the shared experience" (Patton, 2015, p. 116). This type of analysis was appropriate for this study since we were concerned with understanding the experiences of child protective caseworkers, concerning the use of humor. Sanders (1982) reviews that this type of analysis requires the researcher to conduct in-depth examinations. Furthermore, that "it is better to ask fewer questions and to probe them intensively than it is to ask many questions assuming that more questions will yield more data" (Sanders, 1982, p. 356).

As previously mentioned, this study is also a heuristic inquiry, which is a form of phenomenological analysis (Patton, 2015). This form of inquiry seeks to understand the experiences of others, while also incorporating the researcher's (the first author's) experience of the phenomenon. "Heuristic methodology attempts to discover the nature and meaning of phenomenon through internal self-search, exploration, and discovery" (Djuraskovic & Arthur, 2010, p. 1569). This approach requires the researcher to have personal familiarity with the topic of study. This type of inquiry also empowers those who are participants. Patton (2015) refers to those being interviewed, in a heuristic inquiry, as co-researchers. However, there can be challenges to heuristic inquiry in that there can be difficulties with boundaries and the research can be deeply personal (Patton, 2015). Patton (2015) reviews that this approach takes constant shifting between self-dialogue of experiences and the data. At the start of this research, Dr. Landram had planned to integrate her six years of experience and observations with the phenomenon as data. This would have provided for a deeper understanding of how the phenomenon fits into the workplace and how emotions and stress are managed. This would have provided valuable data that might not be able to be observed by a researcher that does not work for the organization. Patton (1990) states that this approach to research provides "high quality data in a social context where people can consider their own views in the context of the views of others" (p. 335). However, the data collected was high quality and informative and shed light into experiences that Dr. Landram had as well. Therefore, she did not heavily add her own experiences in this research. The other framework used for this study was symbolic interaction.

George Herbert Mead (1934) and Herbert Blumer (1969) focused their research on symbolic interaction and how its focus is on the "meaning and interpretation" of individuals (as cited in Patton, 2015, p. 133). This approach focuses on interaction and the group, meaning behind the interaction. Blumer (1969) has three overarching concepts. First of all, symbolic interaction seeks to understand the actions of people towards things, people, and the meaning they attribute to them. Secondly, it seeks to understand the meaning of social interactions. Thirdly, symbolic interaction attempts to understand how things have meanings that are created as a part of a group (Patton, 2015). The symbolic interaction approach to qualitative methods is the "only real way of understanding how people perceive, understand, and interpret the world" (Patton, 2015, p. 133). Therefore, this framework was used to understand the research questions. This is key to understanding the interactive process among child protective caseworkers. This approach aided in understanding how caseworkers communicate, what they perceive as funny, and how they create meaning around humor. Patton (2015) reviews that a core question in this framework is, "What common set of symbols and understanding have emerged in giving meaning to people's interaction?" (p. 133).

Data Collection and Procedures

The data sources that were used for this study were interviews. Dr. Landram originally started an autoethnographic accounting of her previous experiences as a child protective caseworker and as a child protective supervisor to supplement interview data. She did this through recall observation. In addition, she interviewed someone who observed her during her employment at the Office of Children, Youth and Families. Furthermore, she interviewed other people that she worked with at the Office of Children, Youth and Families. This strengthens the data of her own experience with humor at the Office of Children, Youth and Families. Patton (2015) reviews that observations can help a researcher get deeper into sensitive issues and provide a rich description of the inquiry. Child protective caseworkers are guarded about their work experiences when around other individuals that are not employed in the same setting which can cause them to be closed off to expressing themselves to others. Likewise, an Office of Children, Youth and Families office is not an open office where anyone can visit and observe. It requires several clearances, and most offices are locked down and even providers are not typically free to roam all environments in the office. At the time of the interviews, Dr. Landram was doing contract work for the Office of Children, Youth and Families and found that if she expressed that she worked as a child protective caseworker before, the interviewees communicated more freely with her and appeared to be less guarded. Therefore, we think that her autoethnographic experience was an asset to this research, however, she did not use all of her data due to the high quality data collected from participants.

Individual interviews allowed for participants to provide detailed accounts of their own experiences and opinions about their use of humor and gallows humor through one-on-one in-depth responses (Patton, 2015). Specifically, we used a standard open-ended interview in combination with an interview guide approach (Appendix A). Standardized open-ended interviews "consist of a set of questions carefully worded and arranged with the intention of taking each respondent through the same sequence and asking each respondent the same questions with essentially the same words" (Patton, 2015, p. 439). This method was used to provide consistency in the questions which assisted in comparing findings more easily (Patton, 2015). As previously mentioned with phenomenological analysis, it is more efficient to ask fewer questions and do more probing to learn about the studied phenomenon (Sanders, 1982). Therefore, an interview guide approach which allowed for more exploration was utilized. Patton (2015) reviews that using these two approaches together allows us to specify "certain key questions exactly as they must be asked while leaving other items as topics to be explored at the interviewer's discretion" (p. 441). Furthermore, this approach provided us with "flexibility in probing and in determining when it is appropriate to explore certain subjects in greater depth, or even to pose questions about new areas of inquiry that were not originally anticipated in the interview instrument's developed" (Patton, 2015, p. 441). Using both methods together allowed for the data collection to be systematic, however still have a more explorative approach (Patton, 2015).

INTERVIEW GUIDE

- Introduce myself and thank them for taking the time to participate in the interview.
- Review (ensure) they received the letter, IRB approval letter, and that I have the signed consent form.
- Review purpose of study, that the interview is recorded, that they will be confidential and review offer of Amazon card. Also make sure they feel relaxed and know that the study is about humor, etc.
- Ask if they have any questions?

Demographics:

Name/Pseudonym: _____

Gender:_____

Age: _____

Race:_____

Social Class:_____

Married/Single/Children: _____

Education:_____

POSITION AT OFYS: _____

Years at Office of Family and Youth Services/Years employed in position: _____

Geographic area/type (city, country, etc.) of OFYS): _____

How many employees (treatment and intake caseworkers) in your agency:

_____

Questions:

1. What is the funniest thing people have said about your work? (If they have trouble with this frame it like this . . . if comics were making jokes about your job, what would they say?) What are your thoughts about this?
2. If I followed you through a typical day at work, what would I see in regard to the use of humor?
3. Tell me about the funniest thing you have experienced at work? (make sure to find out with whom they are using humor or who was using the humor)
4. What are the jokes/humor you only share with other child welfare workers (inside jokes)?
5. What does gallows humor mean to you (how do you define it)?
6. Tell me about an experience you have had at work (OCYFS) using gallows humor? (get big picture—what occurred before, during, and after).
7. How did you feel right before the use of gallows humor (ensure listening for feeling-level response)?
8. How did you feel right after the use of gallows humor (ensure listening for feeling-level response)?
9. Tell me about a time you experienced gallows humor with the other department or the same department (depending on their response in 6). (get big picture——what occurred before, during, and after and feelings before and after/or why they may not have used humor with them).
10. Can you tell me about a time you used this type of humor with other professionals? (also, if they did not, then explore why they did not).
11. Can you tell me about a time you used this type of humor with others in the community (friends, families, etc.)? (also, if they did not, then explore why they did not).
12. Tell me about a time you used gallows humor by yourself (in your own mind)?
13. Why did you choose not to share this gallows humor with others?
14. Can you tell me about a time you used or witnessed others using humor about the victim?
15. What do you think the positive effects are when you use gallows humor? (if they don't mention individual, group, or organization impacts then may need to probe here more).
16. What do you think the negative effects are when you use gallows humor? (if they don't mention individual, group, or organization impacts then may need to probe here more).
17. How do you think your department (intake or treatment) uses gallows humor similarly? Differently?

18. Is there anything else you would like to share about your experiences or thoughts with humor and/or gallows humor at OCYFS?

That's all the questions I have for you. I really appreciate you taking the time to participate in the interview. Also thank you for the work you do. May I contact you at a future date, if needed for this study?

SAMPLING STRATEGY

This qualitative study used purposeful sampling. Purposeful sampling refers to "selecting information-rich cases to study, cases that by their nature and substance will illuminate the inquiry question being investigated" (Patton, 2015, p. 264). This type of technique allowed for better understanding of how child protective caseworkers experience humor and gallows humor. All participants in this study were over the age of 18 and voluntarily participated. They have previously worked at or are currently employed at an Office of Children, Youth and Families as child protective caseworkers. We first planned to use a combination of snowball and maximum variation sampling strategies to reach the appropriate number and type of employees. However, we only needed to utilize a snowballing strategy. Snowballing sampling, also known as chain sampling, allows for a researcher to start with a few information-rich participant interviews. Then the researcher will ask the participant for other potential participants that have insight into the inquiry (Patton, 2015). This is a good technique for this study because it is difficult to reach child protective workers through formal means. The Office of Children, Youth and Families are not likely to take the time for their staff to participate in research. We had planned to start interviewing 20 participants using this method, however we quickly reached 35 participants.

As mentioned, we also planned to use maximum variation due to its ability to broaden the number of cases, to get a broader concept of the phenomenon under study (Patton, 2015). This would have provided us with more variation in our sample. However, we noticed that the snowballing strategy was able to provide us with some variation. After the initial 20 interviews, we analyzed the data and assessed for variation. When looking for variation we checked for length **[AU: length of time?]**employed by the agency, that both treatment and intake child protective workers are included, and that there is a representation of different races, gender, geographic area, and organizational culture. We were satisfied with the variation and continued with our snowballing technique being aware of the desire to include variation. Dr. Landram interviewed a total of 35 participants.

Dr. Landram interviewed participants that have been employed as a child protective caseworker for a variety of years (between 11 months and 20 years). Since chronic strain has impacts of stress, then there could be variation among new employees and seasoned employees. Likewise, new employees may have different expectations and ways to manage their emotions than those that have been in the field longer. Seasoned employees have also had time to build a relationship with others and learn the duties of their job. As we have already learned, social relationships can be used as a coping mechanism for stress and can inform how emotions should be managed. Furthermore, seasoned employees have had exposure to situations and may have already formed ways to manage those situations, while new employees may be learning how to handle stress and emotions. Therefore, seasoned employees and new employees can utilize humor differently. However, there could also be similarities due to their exposure to seasoned staff. We also ensured that we had a similar number of treatment and intake caseworkers. Since we were seeking to understand the similarities and differences in the two departments and how they utilize humor, it was imperative that we included participants from each department. Another variation we attempted to include was gender and race.

The field is typically made up of female child protective caseworkers. There is no public research, that we are aware of, that reports the percentage of female and male child protective caseworkers. However, most caseworkers in the field are made up of social workers. In 2017, it was noted that 81.2% of social workers are female ("Social Workers," n.d.). Research shows that there are differences in the way women and men experience stress and emotions. Therefore, we did attempt to seek out and include male participants. Three out of 35 participants were male, which is 8.57% of participants in this study. Since about 18.8% of social workers are male and perhaps even a smaller percentage in child welfare, we felt the 3 male caseworkers that were able to participate in the study was sufficient. We also attempted to include participants with diverse racial and ethnic backgrounds in this study, since this may have impacts on the way humor is used. However, most of the participants were Caucasian (31 out of 35) which we acknowledge as a limitation. Another area we wanted diversity in was geographic locations in states and counties, to include small, mid-sized, and large Office of Children, Youth and Families agencies. We were able to obtain representation from 46 different locations in 5 different states across the United States. Typically, larger areas serve more families and receive more referrals for concerns of abuse, and this could impact how an employee experiences stress and humor. The culture of the location the employee works in could also set the stage for how their emotions and stress are to be managed. This entails the size and number of employees employed at the location. Therefore, they could use humor in a different way than other cultures. We continued to do interviews to ensure that these areas were represented until saturation occurred. Saturation occurs when "no new information or themes are observed in the data" (Guest, Bunce & Johnson, 2006, p. 59).

When Dr. Landram contacted a participant to interview, they were provided with an initial email, which informed them about the details of the study. Also included was an informed consent form and a copy of the IRB approval letter. The initial email provided details about the intentions for research and helped participants start to think about the interview topic since sometimes it is easier for individuals to examine a topic like humor over a period of time. The location of the interviews was online through Zoom, a video conferencing platform. Utilizing Zoom was convenient for participants and Dr. Landram and allowed for more time to collect data. Zoom also had the capability of voice recording the interviews. As the interview began, Dr. Landram reviewed the purpose of the study and explained confidently. There was little to no ethical risk to participating in the study since participants were only asked about their experiences. There was no confidential information collected about the clients they serve. Dr. Landram also covered the interview process, provided a time frame for the length of the interview (typically one hour), and reviewed that the interview would be recorded if they consented. In addition, Dr. Landram inquired if she could contact the participant at a future date if needed for this study. Participants were offered a $25.00 gift card from Amazon for the interview. This was to compensate the participants for the time that workers spent doing the interviews. Some participants opted for the gift card, and some declined the gift card.

DATA ANALYSIS METHODS

After Dr. Landram collected data from an interview and completed field notes. She recorded any methodological and analytical comments and notes that she wanted to be reminded of. This helped her identify any issues she may have had during the interview or anything that stood out during the process. The interviews were recorded and transcribed verbatim. Once the data was transcribed, it was imported into NVIVO, which is a computer-assisted qualitative data analysis software (CAQDAS) program. This allowed us to group, pivot, and view respondents' interview data more easily into demographic and coded categories based on meaning. We then looked for themes and commonalities and coded the data using open coding and process coding. Once coding was completed, we developed analytical memos to evaluate emergent themes and assessed the themes in light of the research questions. After the appropriate number of iterations of this process was completed, we assessed internal homogeneity and external heterogeneity of themes. Internal homogeneity refers to making sure that all data within a theme apply to that theme (Patton, 2002). External heterogeneity ensures that there are no over-lapping themes used (Patton, 2002). We then communicated our findings as a cross-case pattern analysis to understand the data. Cross-case pattern analysis takes the data and looks for patterns in content, experiences, and behaviors that are similar and then organizes it under general themes in the findings (Patton, 2015). We also provided participants with a closing email to thank them for their participation in the study.

ASSURANCE OF QUALITY

Dr. Landram utilized an audit trail throughout the research to complete a quality check of the work. An audit trail is a detailed ledger that outlines the data collected and analyzed, as well as both author's reflections on the research. This ledger started at the beginning of the research and concluded through the end of the study. This ledger is in chronological order by dates. "Conducting qualitative research requires considerable reflection on the researcher's ability to make a critical assessment of informants' comments" (Carcary, 2009, p. 12). Therefore, the audit trail kept us accountable for our actions. Another data quality check we used was utilizing clarification or summarization during interviews, so Dr. Landram could understand what the participants were communicating. This ensured that she interpreted what the participant said correctly, decreased any bias she has, and improved credibility (Patton, 2015). We also used debriefing with other professionals. This also increased the credibility of the study because it provided another review of the data (Patton, 2015). These techniques assisted in ensuring the quality of the data that was found.

ETHICAL CONSIDERATIONS

To ensure ethics were considered in this study IRB approval was obtained, an audit trail was utilized, Dr. Landram used clarifying statements throughout the interviews, and the research was overseen by both authors and two other doctors. Before participants in this study were contacted the research proposal was submitted to the Indiana University of Pennsylvania Institutional Review Board (IRB) For the Protection of Human Subjects for approval. Participants in this study voluntarily participated and were over the age of 18 years of age. We ensured steps were taken so that no client contact information was disclosed. Participants were told about confidentiality and the use of pseudonyms for the names of participants and any other identifying information. The level of risk to participants was minimal. Participants were interviewed about their experiences with humor and gallows humor, stress, and emotions they experience while employed at the Office of Children, Youth and Families. Participants were not asked for specific confidential case information or names of clients. Furthermore, participants had the option to disclose as much as they wanted and at any time they could choose to no longer participate. Each interview recording was stored on a password protected electronic device. Participants all had a chance to review their transcribed data and were provided a letter of IRB approval with contact information. As mentioned, Dr. Landram also utilized an audit trail throughout the research to complete a quality check of the work. Another data quality check used was utilizing clarification or summarization during interviews, so we could understand what the participant was communicating. This ensured that Dr. Landram interpreted what the participant said correctly, decreased bias, and improved credibility (Patton, 2015). Throughout interviews clarifying statements were used with participants to ensure proper understanding of participant's statements.

DEMOGRAPHICS

Dr. Landram conducted qualitative interviews with 35 participants from 20 different Office of Children, Youth and Families agencies (Table 1). Of those participants 26 had experience working at one agency, 7 participants had experience working at two different agencies and 2 participants had experience working at three different agencies. The following is a list of the county agencies interviewed, using pseudonyms, along with the number of people interviewed from that location. Since some of the participants worked at more than one agency, there is representation of work experience from 46 locations, rather than 35. Aidville (1), Assistville (1), Believesville (2), Careland (1), Fairland (6), Faith (1), Helpsville (1), Hopesville (2), Kindness (1), Main (4), Manageville (1), Merryland (12), Needsville (4), Refer (1), Savesville (1), Serve (2), SupportsvilleA (1), SupportsvilleB (2), Truth (1), and Wish (1). These agencies are located in five different states throughout the United States in the regions of Northeast, South, and West according to the Census Regions and Divisions of the United States.

Of the 35 participants, 10 worked as a caseworker in the intake department, 7 worked as a caseworker in the treatment department, 16 participants had experience working in both departments (intake and treatment), 1 participant had experience working as a general caseworker, and 1 participant had experience as an intake, treatment, and a general caseworker. For this study we focused on the intake and treatment departments for our third research question: Are there any similarities and/or differences in how intake and treatment employees utilize gallows humor? However, since Dr. Landram was afforded the opportunity to interview two people that had been a general caseworker, they were interviewed and their data is included in this research study as it applied to our research questions. The least amount of time that a participant remained in a department (intake, treatment, or general) was 3 months and the longest time was 16 years. However, the overall range of a career as a child protective caseworker (intake and treatment) ranged from 11 months to 20 years.

A majority (31 out of 35) racially identified themselves as Caucasian, 2 identified themselves as being Hispanic, and 2 identified as being African American. The participants were mainly female (32 out of 35), and they ranged from 23 years of age to 54 years of age at the time of their interview. A majority (32 out of 35) of the participants identified economically as being middle class, 1 identified as being upper class, and 2 reported they were unsure of their economic status. Participants also ranged from being single, in a committed relationship, engaged, married, and being separated. Furthermore, some of the participants had no children and some had children and/or stepchildren.

STRENGTHS OF THE STUDY

As previously discussed, to ensure ethics were considered we obtained IRB approval, utilized an audit trail, used clarify statements throughout interviews, and the research had oversight. These steps also increased the strength of the study by decreasing error and having feedback for more effective methods to do research. We were able to interview 35 participants and have representation from 46 different Office of Children and Youth Agencies. The variation of locations is a strength of this study because it considers different geographic locations. Furthermore, the main strength of this research is that it: 1) Affirms the literature about humor theory, stress theory in relation to humor, and the sociology of emotions in relation to humor; 2) extends literature by incorporating impacts of humor in relation to stress and emotions at the organizational level; and 3) extends policy implications.

LIMITATION OF THE STUDY

As with any social research there are weaknesses and limitations to this study. The limitations of this study are aspects of the approaches (heuristic inquiry,

Table 1: Participant Demographics

Gender: F = Female, M= Male

Race: AA= African American, C= Caucasian, H= Hispanic

Social Class: M=Middle Class, U= unsure, UC=upper class

Relationship Status: E=Engaged, M=Married, S=Single, SE= Separated

Department time at CYS: I=Intake, G= general, T=Treatment

Pseudonym	Gender	Age	Race	Social Class	Relationship Status	Children	Education	Department time at CYS	CYS Pseudonym
1 Abigail	F	28	C	NP	S	0	Social Work (B)	Intake 3yrs	Merryland County
2 Ann	F	37	C	M	M	2	Social Work (B)	Treatment 5 yrs.	Fairland County
3 Ashley	F	32	C	M	M	2	Social Work (B)	Intake 1 yr. and Treatment 1 ½ = 2yrs	Fairland County
4 Betty	F	33	C	M	M	0	Criminal Justice (B)	Ongoing 3 yrs.	Merryland County
5 Charlotte	F	25	C	M	S	0	Social Work (M)	Intake 5yrs	Merryland County
6 Christy	F	48	C	M	S	2	Psychology (B)	Intake 5yrs. and Treatment 2yrs, other 13 yrs. = 20 yrs. at CYS	Fairland County
7 Crystal	F	32	C	M	M	2	Rehabilitative Science (B)	Intake (2yrs and 9 months) and Treatment (2 months) = 2 yrs. and 11 months	Helpsville County
8 Dana	F	31	AA	M	S	0	Psychology (B)	Treatment -7 ½ yrs.	Aidville County / Main County

Pseudonym	Gender	Age	Race	Social Class	Relationship Status	Children	Education	Department time at CYS	CYS Pseudonym
9 Evelyn	F	54	C	M	M	3	Social Work (B) and Social Service Administration (M)	4–5 yrs.(I) and 2 months(T) = 4–5 yrs. and 2 months	Merryland County
10 Ella	F	49	C	M	S	2(bio) 1(step)	Special Education (B)	Intake – 2 ½ yrs.	Hopesville County
11 Gina	F	44	C	M	M	2(bio) 2(step)	Business Management (B) and Human Services Management and special education (M)	Intake - 25 yrs. on social service (she is unsure how long at CYS)	Hopesville County
12 Harper	F	23	H	M	S	0	Criminal Justice (B)	Intake and Treatment 1 yr.(I) and 1 yr.(T) = 2 yrs.	Merryland County
13 Hazel	F	33	C	M	M	4	Sociology (B) and Counseling Psychology (M)	Treatment 2 yrs.(T) and 2 yrs. (other) = 2 yrs. CW (4 yrs. at CYS	Main County
14 Isabella	F	32	C	M	M	0	Early Childhood Education (B)	Intake	Main County
15 Jade	F	28	C	M	S	0	MSW	1 1/2 yrs.(G)	SupportsvilleA County

Pseudonym	Gender	Age	Race	Social Class	Relationship Status	Children	Education	Department time at CYS	CYS Pseudonym
16 Jewel	F	33	C	U	M	1	Criminal Justice (B)	6 yrs. and 3 months 5 months or more (I), 5 yrs. (T), 1 yr. (G), 5 yrs. (other) = 12 years	Careland County / Main County
17 Kelly	F	35	C	M	M	3	Elementary and Early Childhood Education (B) and Social Work (M)	Intake and Treatment 5 yrs.(I) and 3 yrs. (T) = 8yrs	Savesville County / Wish County
18 Lily	F	48	C	M	S	0	MSW	Intake and Treatment 2 1/2 years(I) and 3 years(T) = 51/2yrs	Needsville County
19 Mandy	F	26	C	M	S	0	Social Work (B) and Legal Studies (M)	Intake and Treatment 5 yrs. and 6 months (I) and 6 months(T) = 6yrs	Needsville County / Merryland County
20 Naomi	F	30	C	M	M	1	Social Work (M)	Intake and Treatment 5 years(I) and 3 years(T) = 8 years	Merryland County

Pseudonym	Gender	Age	Race	Social Class	Relationship Status	Children	Education	Department time at CYS	CYS Pseudonym
21 Nora	F	26	C	M	S	0	Social Work (M)	Intake and Treatment 7 months(I) and little over 4 yrs. (T) = 5 yrs.	Assistville County / Merryland County
22 Novah	F	28	C	M	S	0	Social Work (B)	Ongoing 1 ½ yrs.	Needsville County
23 Olivia	F	27	C	M	S	0	Social Work (B)	Treatment 5yrs	Fairland County
24 Peter	M	30	C	M	S	0	Criminal Justice (B) and Public Administration (M)	Intake 3 yrs.	Merryland County
25 Phoebe	F	46	C	M	M	3	MSW	Intake and Treatment 9 yrs.(I), 1 yr.(T), 3 1/2 yrs. (other) = 10 yrs. CW (13 1/2 yrs. at CYS)	Kindness County
26 Quinton	M	35	C	M	M	0	Criminal Justice (B)	Intake and Treatment 1 yr.(I) and 6 yrs.(T) = 7 yrs.	Believesville County
27 Rose	F	48	C	M	M	1	Social Work (M)	Intake and General 16 yrs.(I), 3 yrs.(G), 1 yr. (other) = 20 years	Needsville County
28 Sabrina	F	26	C	M	E	0	Rehabilitation in Human Services (B)	Intake 2yrs	Merryland County

Pseudonym	Gender	Age	Race	Social Class	Relationship Status	Children	Education	Department time at CYS	CYS Pseudonym
29 Sophia	F	23	C	M	S	0	Social Work (B)	Intake 1 yr.	SupportsvilleB County
30 Steven	M	40	C	M	Sep	0	Secondary Education (B)	Intake 11 months	SupportsvilleB County / Fairland County
31 Susan	F	40	H	M	E	2	Education and Sociology (B)	Intake and Treatment 4 yrs.(I) and 5 yrs.(T) = 9 yrs.	Merryland County / Refer County / Manageville County
32 Toni	F	34	C	M	M	0	Social Work (B)	Treatment 10 yrs.	Serve County / Faith County / Truth County
33 Trish	F	36	AA	M	M	1(step)	Psychology(B) and Public Safety (M)	Intake and Treatment 2-3 yrs.(I) and 1 yr.(T) = 3–4 yrs.	Merryland County
34 Violet	F	32	C	NP	M	1(bio) 2(step)	Criminal Justice (B)	Intake and Treatment 5yrs(I) and 1yr(T) = 6 yrs.	Believesville County / Serve County
35 Zoe	F	52	C	M	M	2(bio) 2(step)	Psychology (B)	Intake7 ½ years	Fairland County

symbolic interactionist, and phenomenological approaches). This includes the need to be cognizant of one's own experiences, the study not being generalizable, and a lack of focus on negative aspects of humor. In addition, there are limitations to qualitative research, such as error of researcher, replication, and the volunteer status of participants.

This study started out heavily using the approach of heuristic inquiry, which has strengths, but also has some limitations. It takes caution on the researcher's part when interviews are conducted. The researcher needs to be careful not to enforce one's own experience on the participant (Djuraskovic & Arthur, 2010). A thorough review of the researcher's own experiences is needed, which means that we had to ensure that Dr. Landram did not transfer her own experiences onto participants. Even though her experiences are not noted heavily in the research, it is important to be aware that she had her own experiences at child welfare that could be transferred onto those interviewed. Since the researcher's bias could influence how they hear and perceive the data they collect (Djuraskovic & Arthur, 2010). We had to utilize methods to address this. Therefore, to ensure transparency, Dr. Landram used an audit trail, clarifying statements, recorded the interviews, completed field notes, and we coded the data more than once and had it reviewed by other professional researchers.

This study also comes from the perspectives of symbolic interactionist and phenomenological approaches. The symbolic interactionist approach to humor is critiqued because the studies are typically ethnographic and are not able to be generalizable. This study incorporates interviews from caseworkers at different organizations, which can offset some of this concern. However, this study is still not generalizable because the study researched Office of Children, Youth and Families caseworkers that have their own views of reality. Different demographics and cultures could impact how employees perceive and utilize humor. Therefore, different child welfare caseworkers may have different experiences. We attempted to address this area by ensuring variation in the data, however we were unable to ensure to include some variations, like race and gender. Therefore, this is still a limitation of this study. The phenomenological approach to humor is critiqued because it does not take into account negative aspects of humor and can lack clarity on how it contributes to empirical research. This research study assesses the negative and positive aspects of using gallows humor and therefore can diminish some of these concerns. We also attempt to demonstrate how the impacts of humor actually does contribute to research.

Patton (2002) reviews that some limitations of qualitative research included errors on the researcher's ability to recall and assumptions that the researcher makes about responses. In order to minimize this limitation Dr. Landram recorded and transcribed the interviews verbatim and reviewed the data on more than one occasion. Furthermore, member checks were used to clarify any ambiguous response a participant reported during the interview. Another area of limitation in qualitative interviews is that they are hard to replicate (Marshall & Rossman, 1999). An interview-guided approach was utilized to assist in this area. However, this is still a limitation of the study because the exact replication could not be met. Furthermore, all participants in this study were volunteers and were willing to talk about their stress, emotions, and use of humor and gallows humor. It is possible that other employees who did not have interviews could have shared similar or different experiences.

FUTURE RESEARCH

Further research should be done on general child protective caseworkers, other frontline responders, and more interviews that include more diverse child welfare caseworkers.

Future research should take into consideration assessing general child protective caseworkers. This would be informative because they perform both the intake and treatment department tasks. This could assist in gaining a better understanding about humor, emotions, and stress, since they experience the same job roles and elicit different emotions from their clients depending on which stage they are with the family.

Further research should be conducted of other frontline responders such as EMTs, coroners, and military. Research has predominantly focused on police and nurses. This could broaden information about humor, emotions, and stress. Research could compare the similarities and differences among these job roles. This could also assist in gaining a better understanding about how stress theory, sociology of emotions, and humor are connected and experienced by a variety of individuals in different job fields.

Another area that future research could expand on is interviews with more male caseworkers and more racially diverse male and female caseworkers. This would aid in understanding how gender and race experience stress, emotions, and humor. Since these factors heavily influence the stress experience and how they manage emotions it could have varying implications on how humor is utilized. It could also shed light on how males navigate a career in child welfare. In my findings, Peter noted that he felt uncomfortable at times and females were cruder with their jokes than what he had heard in male locker rooms. Understanding these impacts on males and how they address their humor, in relation to comfort levels and fear of repercussion for using humor with females would make for informative research that can extend literature.

SUMMARY

This qualitative approach was appropriate for the research questions because we were concerned with understanding how child protective caseworkers experience gallows humor at work. We assume that people all have different realities of how they experience emotion, stress, and humor within the Office of Children, Youth and Families. We used a phenomenological analysis, heuristic inquiry (to a degree), and symbolic interaction as my research design. The combination of these three approaches directly shed light on understanding the research questions in this study. The data consisted of standard open-ended interviews in combination with an interview- guide approach, with current and previous child protective caseworkers. This was done through the purposeful sampling techniques of snowballing. This allowed us to assess child protective caseworkers and provide fundamental knowledge through analysis. Dr. Landram recorded her reflection into field notes and once the data was transcribed, it was imported into NVIVO. We then coded the data and analyzed the data through memo techniques. The findings were then documented in the study by categorizing it into themes with the supporting data.

References

Altenau, M. (2010). *The role of humor in depth psychology: A phenomenological study.* Retrieved from ProQuest. UMI 3475571.

Alvarado, G. E. (2013). *Gallows humor as a resiliency factor among urban firefighters with specific implications on prevalence rates of PTSD* (Doctoral dissertation). Retrieved from ProQuest. 3552414.

Anderson, D. G. (2000). Coping Strategies and Burnout Among Veteran Child Protection Workers. Child Abuse and Neglect, 24(6), 839-848. https://doi.org/10.1016/S0145-2134(00)00143-5

Atkinson, C. (2006). Self-deprecation and the habit of laughter. *Florida Philosophical Review, XV*(1), 19–36. https://cah.ucf.edu/fpr/article/self-deprecation-and-the-habit-of-laughter/

Barsade, S. G., & Gibson, D. E. (2007). Why does affect matter in organizations? *Academy of Management Perspectives, 21*(1), 36–59.

Billig, M. (2005). *Laughter and ridicule: Towards a social critique of humor.* London: Sage.

Blumer, H. (1969). *Symbolic interactionism: Perspective and method.* Berkeley: University of California Press.

Buchanan M., & Keats, P. (2011). Coping with traumatic stress in journalism: A critical ethnographic study. *International Journal of Psychology, 46*(2), 127–135. https://doi.org/10.1080/00207594.2010.532799.

Camus, A. (1990). The myth of Sisyphus. London: Penguin.

Carcary, M. (2009). The research audit trail – enhancing trustworthiness in qualitative inquiry. The Electronic Journal of Business Research Methods, 7(1), 11-24., 7(1), 11-24. Retrieved from https://www.researchgate.net/publication/228667678_The_Research_Audit_Trial-Enhancing_Trustworthiness_in_Qualitative_Inquiry.

Child Welfare Information Gateway. (2013). *How the child welfare system works.* Washington, DC: U.S. Department of Health and Human Services, Children's Bureau. Retrieved from: https://www.childwelfare.gov/pubPDFs/cpswork.pdf#page=1&view=Introduction

Child Welfare Information Gateway. (2019). *Collaboration among public agencies.* Washington, DC: U.S. Department of Health and Human Services, Children's

Bureau. Retrieved from: https://www.childwelfare.gov/topics/management/practice-improvement/collaboration/public/

Children's Bureau: An Office of the Administration for Children & Families [Website]. Retrieved August 9, 2019, from: https://www.acf.hhs.gov/cb/about/history

Conrad, D., & Kellar-Guenther, Y. (2006). Compassion fatigue, burnout, and compassion satisfaction among Colorado child protection workers. *Child Abuse and Neglect, 30,* 1071–1080.

Cooper, C. L., & Dewe, P. (2004). *Stress: A brief history.* Malden, MA: Blackwell.

Coser, R. (1960). Laughter among colleagues: A study of the social functions of humor among the staff of a mental hospital. *Psychiatry, 23*(1), 81–95.

Coughlin, J. J. (2002). *Gallows humor and its use among police officers* (Doctoral dissertation). James Madison University, Harrisonburg, VA. Retrieved from ProQuest Information & Learning.

Craun, S. W., & Bourke, M. L. (2014). The use of humor to cope with secondary traumatic stress. *Journal of Child Sexual Abuse, 23*(7), 840–852.

Craun, S. W., & Bourke, M. L. (2015). Is laughing at the expense of victims and offenders a red flag? Humor and secondary traumatic stress. *Journal of Child Sexual Abuse, 24*(5), 592–601.

Creswell, J. W. (2009). *Research design: Qualitative, quantitative, and mixed methods approaches.* Los Angeles: Sage.

Davis, M. (1993). *What's so Funny? The Comic Conception of Culture and Society.* Chicago: University of Chicago Press.

Deadpan. (n.d.). In *Oxford Learner's Dictionaries.* Retrieved from: https://www.oxfordlearnersdictionaries.com/us/definition/american_english/deadpan

Djuraskovic, I., & Arthur, N. (2010). Heuristic inquiry: A personal journey of acculturation and identity construction. *The Qualitative Report, 15*(5), 1569–1593.

Dundes, A. (1987). *Cracking jokes: Studies of sick humor cycles and stereotypes.* Berkeley: Ten Speed Press.

Dunkel-Schetter, C., & Bennett. T. L. (1990). Differentiating the cognitive and behavioral aspects of social support. In G. R. Pierce (Ed.), *Social support: An interactional view* (pp. 267–296). New York: Wiley.

Emerson, J. (1969). Negotiating the serious import of humor. *Sociometry, 32*(2), 169–181.

Endler, N. S., & Parker, J. D. A. (1994). Assessment of multidimensional coping: Task, emotion, and avoidance strategies . Psychological Assessment, 6, 50–60.

Farester, E. L. (2016). *Assessing stress and coping among federal probation officers* (Doctoral dissertation). Retrieved from ProQuest. 10241441.

Ferguson, M. A., & Ford, T. E. (2008). Disparagement humor: A theoretical and empirical review of psychoanalytic, superiority, and social identity theories. *Humor: International Journal of Humor Research, 21*(3), 283–312.

Fields, J., Copp, M., & Kleinman, S. (2006). Symbolic interactionism, inequality, and emotions. In Jan Stets & Jonathan H. Turner (Ed.), *Handbook of the sociology of emotions* (pp. 155–178). Boston, MA: Springer.

Folkman, S. (1984). Personal control and stress and coping processes: A theoretical analysis. *Journal of Personality and Social Psychology, 46*(4), 839–852.

Folkman, S., Lazarus, R. S., Dunkel-Schetter, C., DeLongis, A., & Gruen, R. J. (1986). The dynamics of a stressful encounter: Cognitive appraisal, coping, and encounter outcomes. *Journal of Personality and Social Psychology, 50*(5), 992–1003.

Francis, L. E. (1994). Laughter, the best mediation: Humor as emotion management in interaction. *Symbolic Interaction, 17*(2), 147–163.

Freud, S. (1976). *Jokes and their relation to the unconscious* (Ed. James Strachey and Angela Richards). London: Penguin. (Original work published 1905.)

Goffman, E. (1974). *Frame analysis: An essay in the organization of experience.* Boston: Northeastern University Press.

Gruner, C. (1978). *Understanding laughter: The working of wit and humor.* Chicago: Nelson-Hall.

Guest, G., Bunce, A., & Johnson, L. (2006). How many interviews are enough?: An experiment with data saturation and variability. *Field Method, 18*(1), 59–82.

Heifetz, R. A. (1998). *Leadership without easy answers.* Cambridge, MA: Belknap Press of Harvard University Press.

Heverling, M. (2011). *Burnout prevalence and prevention in a state child welfare agency* (Bachelor's degree). Retrieved from Social Work Theses, 69.

Hochschild, A. R. (1979). Emotion work, feeling rules, and social structure. *The American Journal of Sociology, 85*(3), 551–575.

Hochschild, A. R. (2003). *The managed heart: Commercialization of human feeling.* Berkeley and Los Angeles, CA: University of California Press.

Howell, A. C. (2008). *Protecting the self: An ethnographic study of emotion management among child protective investigators* (Master's thesis). Retrieved from University of South Florida Scholar Commons.

Johnco, C., Salloum, A., Olson, K. R., & Edwards, L. M. (2014). Child welfare workers' perspectives on contributing factors to retention and turnover: Recommendations for improvement. *Children and Youth Services Review, 47*, 397–407.

Johnson, A. L. (2007). *Organizational cynicism and occupational stress in police officers* (Doctoral dissertation). Retrieved from ProQuest. 3302892.

Karasek, R. A. (1979). Job demands, job decision latitude, and mental strain: Implications for job re-design. *Administrative Science Quarterly, 24*(2), 285–308.

Kuipers, G. (2008). The sociology of humor. In Victor Raskin (Ed.), *The Primer of Humor Research* (pp. 365–402). Berlin/New York: Mouton de Gruyter.

Lazarus, R. S. (1999). *Stress and emotion: A new synthesis.* New York, NY: Springer.

Lois, J. (2003). *Heroic efforts: The emotional culture of search and rescue volunteers.* New York, New York: University Press.

Lockyer, S., & Pickering, M. (2005). *Beyond the joke: The limits of humour.* Basingstoke: Palgrave.

Macduff, N. (2005). *The Jossey-Bass handbook of nonprofit leadership and management, 2nd edition: Principles of Training for Volunteers and Employees.* San Francisco, CA: Jossey-Bass.

Maden, J. (2020, April). Thomas Nagel on why humor is the best response to life's absurdity. *Philosophy Break.* https://philosophybreak.com/articles/thomas-nagel-why-humor-best-stance-towards-life-absurdity/

Marshall, C., & Rossman, G. B. (1999). *Designing qualitative research* (3rd ed.). Thousand Oaks, CA: Sage.

Maxwell, J. C. (2005). Emerging research on methamphetamine. *Current Opinion in Psychiatry, 18*(3), 235–242. doi:10.1097/01.yco.0000165592.52811.84.

Mead, G.H. (1934). *Mind, Self, and Society from the Standpoint of a Social Behaviorist.* University of Chicago Press: Chicago.

Meerlo, J. (1966). The biology of laughter. *Psychoanalytic Review, 53*, 25–44.

Mesmer-Magnus, J., Glew, D. J., & Chockalingam, V. (2012). A meta-analysis of positive humor in the workplace. *Journal of Managerial Psychology, 27*(2), 155–190.

Mirowsky, J., & Ross, C.E. (2003). *Social causes of psychological distress.* New York: Aldine de Gruyter.

Monro, D. H. (1988). Theories of humor. In L. Behrens & L. J. Rosen (Eds.), *Writing and reading across the curriculum* (3rd ed.) (pp. 349–355). Glenview, IL: Scott, Foresman and Company.

Morreall, J. (1983). *Taking laughter seriously.* Albany: State University of New York Press.

Morreall, J. (1987). *The philosophy of laughter and humor.* Albany: State University of New York Press.

Mulkay, M. (1988). *On humor: Its nature and its place in modern society.* New York: Blackwell Inc.

Nagel, T. (1971). The Absurd. The Journal of Philosophy, 68(20), 716-727.

National Association of Social Workers. (2023). *Code of Ethics.* https://www.socialworkers.org/About/Ethics/Code-of-Ethics

Obrdlik, A. J. (1942). Gallows humor—A sociological phenomenon. *American Journal of Sociology, 47*(5), 709–716.

Patton, M. Q. (1990). *Qualitative evaluation and research methods.* Newbury Park, CA: Sage.

Patton, M. Q. (2002). *Qualitative research and evaluation methods.* Thousand Oaks, CA: Sage Publications.

Patton, M. Q. (2015). *Qualitative research and evaluation methods.* Thousand Oaks, CA: Sage Publications.

Pogrebin, M. R., & Poole, E. D. (1988). Humor in the briefing room: A study of the strategic uses of humor among police. *Journal of Contemporary Ethnography, 17*(2), 183–210.

Regehr, C., & Bober, T. (2005). *In the line of fire: Trauma in the emergency services.* New York: Oxford University Press.

Regehr, C., Goldberg, G., & Hughes, J. (2002). Exposure to human tragedy, empathy, and trauma in ambulance paramedics. *American Journal of Orthopsychiatry, 72*(4), 505–513.

Riolli, L., & Savicki, V. (2010). Coping effectiveness and coping diversity under traumatic stress. *International Journal of Stress Management, 17,* 97–113. doi:10.1037/a0018041

Roth, G. L., & Vivona, B. (2010). Mirth and murder: Crime scene investigation as a work context for examining humor applications. *Human Resource Development Review, 9,* 314–332. doi:10.1177/1534484310379958

Rowe, A., & Regehr, C. (2010). Whatever gets you through today: An examination of cynical humor among emergency service professionals. *Journal of Loss and Trauma, 15*(5), 448–464.

Ruchti, L. C. (2012). *Catheters, slurs, and pickup lines: Professional intimacy in hospital nursing.* Philadelphia: Temple University Press.

Salloum, A., Kondrat S. C., Johnco, C., & Olson K. R. (2015). The role of self-care on compassion satisfaction, burnout and secondary trauma among child welfare workers. *Children and Youth Services Review, 49*(C), 54–61.

Sanders, P. (1982). A new way of viewing organizational research. *The Academy of Management Review, 7*(3), 353–360.

Schein, Edgar H. (2004). The Concept of Organizational Culture: Why Bother? In J. Shafritz, J. Ott & Y. Jang (Eds.), *Classics of organizational theory* (7th ed., pp. 349–360). Boston, MA: Wadsworth.

Scott, T. (2007). Expression of humour by emergency personnel involved in sudden deathwork. *Mortality, 12*(4), 350–364.

Shin, J. (2011). Client violence and its negative impacts on work attitudes of child protection workers compared to community service workers. *Journal of Interpersonal Violence, 26*(16), 3338–3360.

Smith, D. E. (1990/2007). The conceptual practices of power. In C. J. Calhoun, J. Gerteis, J. Moody, S. Pfaff & I. Virk (Eds.), *Contemporary sociological theory* (2nd ed., pp. 318–326). Malden, MA: Blackwell Publishing. (Reprinted from: The conceptual practices in power: A feminist sociology of knowledge, pp. 12–19, 21–27, by D. E. Smith, 1990, Boston, MA: Northeastern University Press.)

Social Workers. (n.d.). Retrieved from: https://datausa.io/profile/soc/211020#about

Speier, H. (1998). Wit and politics: An essay on laughter and power. *American Journal of Sociology, 103*(5), 1352–1401.

Stalker, C. A., Mandell, D., Frensch, K., Harvey, C., & Wright, M. (2007). Child welfare workers who are exhausted yet satisfied with their jobs: How do they do it? *Child and Family Social Work, 12,* 182–191.

Steele, S. F., Scarisbrick-Hauser, A., & Hauser, W. J. (Eds.). (1999). *Solution-centered sociology; Addressing problems through applied sociology.* Lanham, MD: Altamira Press.

Taris, T. W., & Schreurs, P. G. (2009). Well-being and organizational performance: An organizational-level test of the happy-productive worker hypothesis. *Work & Stress, 23*(2), 120–136.

Thoits, P. A. (1989). The sociology of emotions. *Annual Review of Sociology, 15,* 317–342.

Thoits, P. A. (1995). Stress, coping, and social support processes: Where are we? what next?. *Journal of Health and Social Behavior* (Extra Issue), 53–79.

Thorson, J. A. (1993). Did you ever see a hearse go by? Some thought on gallows humor. *Journal of American Culture, 16,* 17–24.

Turcotte, S. A. (2017). *After the call: First responders' coping strategies* (Doctoral dissertation). Retrieved from ProQuest. 10624195.

van Wormer, K., & Boes, M. (1997). Humor in the emergency room: A social work perspective. *Health Social Work, 22*(2), 87–92. doi:10.1093/hsw/22.2.87

Vinokur, A., & Selzer, M. L. (1975). Desirable versus undesirable life events: Their relationship to stress and mental distress. *Journal of Personality and Social Psychology, 32*(2), 329–337.

Vivona, B. D. (2013). *Was that levity or livor mortis? Crime scene investigators.* Perspectives on humor and work (Doctoral dissertation). Retrieved from ProQuest. 3552300.

Vivona, B. D. (2014). Humor functions within crime scene investigations: Group dynamics, stress, and the negotiation of emotions. *Police Quarterly, 17*(2), 127–149.

Vogler, W. B. (2011). *Humor and work: Toward a more contextual understanding of humor in the workplace* (Doctoral dissertation). Retrieved from ProQuest. UMI 3481650.

Watson, K. (2011). Gallows humor in medicine. *The Hastings Center Report, 41*(5), 37–45.

West, A. L. (2015). Associations among attachment style, burnout, and compassion fatigue in health and human service workers: A systematic review. *Journal of Human Behavior in the Social Environment, 25*(6), 571–590.

Wharton, A. (2009). The sociology of emotional labor. *Annual Review of Sociology 35,* 147–165.

Wright, R., Powell, M. B., & Ridge, D. (2006). Child abuse investigation: An in-depth analysis of how police officers perceive and cope with daily work challenges. *Policing: An International Journal of Police Strategies and Management, 29*(3), 498–512.

Zijderveld, A. (1982). *Reality in a looking-glass: Rationality through an analysis of traditional folly.* London: Routledge and Kegan Paul.

Index

distress, 29–30, 91, 100
divorce, 57
doll pranks, 40–41, 83, 88
drug abuse, 18, 41, 63, 78, 80; by
    clients, 28, 51–52, 69
drugs, 3–6, 41; heroin, 75; marijuana,
    78, 80; methamphetamines, 4–5, 15,
    42–43, 69. *see also* alcohol
drug tests, 28, 51

eating, disordered, 11, 17
Emergency Medical Services, 5, 15, 27
emotional beliefs, 31
emotional deviance, 102
emotional exhaustion, 90, 99
emotional labor, 13–14, 22, 31–34, 92,
    96–98
emotion-focused strategies, 90–91, 93
emotion management, 18, 108;
    definition, 31; employee, 13–14,
    32–35, 62, 74, 97–98, 100; group,
    81–82, 88, 92, 93, 103; individual,
    88, 92, 93, 100, 103
emotions of referred families, 11, 17
emotion vocabularies, 31
emotion work, 54–55
empathy, 14, 33, 99, 101
employee emotions, 97
employee roles, 13–14, 98–99
employee self-esteem, 93
ethics, 29, 59, 66–71, 95. *see also*
    professional ethics
exercise, 11, 17–18
exhaustion. *see* burnout
existentialism, 20–21

false allegations, 49
fear, 1–5, 74–76, 84; of judgment, 60,
    63–64. *see also* danger; safety
feces, 3, 43, 47, 49
federal child and family legislation, 7
feeling rules, 31, 32
films, 23
fiscal workers, 7
flight attendants, 13, 32–33, 97–98

foster system, 7–8, 31
framing rules, 32
Freud, Sigmund: *Jokes and their
    Relation to the Unconscious,* 24, 88
friendships, 60. *see also* bonding
functionalism, 24, 25, 93

gallows humor, 37; as a coping
    mechanism, 10, 30; definitions, 18,
    26; as offensive, 26–27; reframing
    traumatic situations, 24, 90, 94; in
    research, 12, 14. *see also* coping
    mechanisms; intake caseworkers'
    use of humor; monitoring; offensive
    humor; taboo topics
games, 37–38, 41, 88, 92. *see also*
    pranks
gangbangers, 75, 89
gang rape, 52
gendered conflict, 64
gender expectations, 31
Goffman, Erving, 55
group cohesion, 59–61, 92, 95–96, 103
group culture, 25, 26–27, 31, 38, 92–93
group dynamics, 65, 88, 92–94, 96, 104
guilt, 2, 68–69, 102
gun violence, 50, 75–77

harassment, 97
harms of humor. *see* negative impacts
    of humor
"The Haven," 82, 97, 100
headlice, 4, 53
healthcare providers, 26
*Heroic Efforts: The Emotional Culture
    of Search and Rescue Volunteers*
    (Lois), 97
heroin, 75
heroism, 2, 20–21, 105
heuristic inquiry, 107–108
hierarchy, 24–25
high caseloads, 10, 18–20, 37, 49, 58
Hochschild, Arlie Russell: *The Managed
    Heart,* 13, 32, 97–98
homes, dirty, 43, 64, 79, 88

About the Authors

Lisa N. Landram is a journalist specializing in Public Safety at the *Daily News-Record* in Virginia. Dr. Landram is also the Field Director of the Master of Science in Psychology program and adjunct professor at Bridgewater College. Her research focuses on human and organizational behavior, emotions, stress, and humor.

Christian Vaccaro is professor of sociology at Indiana University of Pennsylvania. Dr. Vaccaro's research interests are in sociological social psychology. Specifically, he has published and presented multiple research manuscripts that link together by their insights into how patterns of interactions between people in real-world settings influence emotions, identities, and behaviors.